Monday morning

First thing Monday morning

WEEKLY MEDITATIONS FOR
YOUR WORK WEEK

DIANNA BOOHER

Publishers Since 1798

THOMAS NELSON PUBLISHERS

Nashville

Published in Nashville, Tennessee, by Thomas Nelson, Inc., Publishers, and distributed in Canada by Word Communications, Ltd., Richmond, British Columbia, and in the United Kingdom by Word (UK), Ltd., Milton Keynes, England.

Unless otherwise noted, Scripture quotations are from the NEW KING JAMES VERSION of the Bible. Copyright © 1979, 1980, 1982, Thomas Nelson, Inc., Publishers.

Scripture quotations noted CEV are from the CONTEMPORARY ENGLISH VERSION of the Bible © 1991 by the American Bible Society. Used by permission.

Scripture quotations noted NRSV are from the NEW REVISED STANDARD VERSION of the Bible © 1989 by the Division of Christian Education of the National Council of Churches of Christ in the U.S.A. All rights reserved.

Scripture quotations noted TLB are from *The Living Bible* (Wheaton, Illinois: Tyndale House Publishers, 1971) and are used by permission.

Library of Congress Cataloging-in-Publication Data

Booher, Dianna Daniels.

First thing Monday morning / Dianna Booher.

p. cm.

ISBN 0-8407-4569-9 (pbk.)

1. Devotional calendars.   2. Business — Religious aspects —
Christianity — Meditations.   I. Title.

BV4810.586   1993

242'.2 — dc20

92-35207

CIP

Printed in the United States of America

1 2 3 4 5 6 7 - 98 97 96 95 94 93

In memory of my grandparents:
Albert and Anna Schronk
and
Allen and Mabel Daniels

And, once again, to my parents:
Alton and Opal Daniels

All of whom taught and lived
most of the truths on these pages

Contents

Acknowledgments

Several of the quotations used in this book are taken from two excellent collections: *A Treasury of Quotations on Christian Themes*, compiled by Carroll E. Simcox (Seabury Press, 1975), and *The New Dictionary of Thoughts*, compiled by Tyron Edwards, D.D. (Doubleday, 1960).

Introduction

"Stocks plummet. Harrison wins the mayor's race. The storms continue with major flooding in the area. Stay tuned at 10:00 for details."

So goes the nightly TV news commentator with weather and business briefs for harried and hurried business people. We get so accustomed to the pace—fast foods, fast cars, overnight mail, one-day printing, and two-hour laundry service—that sometimes we have little time or energy left for God. Particularly, between eight and five.

A century ago, gathering the family around the table for Bible reading was not an unfamiliar scene. Today it is. Frequently the Bible is the last thing we include in our reading schedule—some time after the newspaper, mail, magazine, professional journal, and file notes for tomorrow's meeting.

But approaching our work environment without hearing God's voice can be as disappointing, even disastrous, as striking out on vacation without the weather forecasts for our destination. Every time I read through Proverbs particularly, I become more aware just how practical—and essential—the Bible is for everyday business situations.

First Thing Monday Morning focuses attention on what God might say to us if He briefed us weekly on bringing our Christianity to the office.

Whether you're an employee or employer, I hope these fifty-two business briefs help you start each week with God's measure of success.

Dianna Booher

Humor in the Boardroom

A merry heart does good, like medicine,
But a broken spirit dries the bones.
(Prov. 17:22)

People show their character and their Christianity by what they think is funny. And sooner or later, we must deal with all forms of humor popping up in the workplace: repartee, wit, irony, cynicism, jokes, pranks, and ridicule. Most of us can quote the first half of the above proverb, but we often have not placed equal emphasis on the last portion. Humor can build people up or knock them down, ease tension or create hostility, make a serious disagreement lighter or make a minor conflict unbearable, attract people to our faith or cause them to run from it.

A sense of humor can be sunshine in a windowless office or a reward during an economic downturn. First of all, it helps us step back from the seriousness of a situation and put difficulties into perspective. Eleanor Roosevelt once observed that without the ability to treat serious things lightly after the heavy thinking is done and the decisions reached, no person could long carry out the job of President of the United States.

During Ronald Reagan's presidency, his humor did more to calm the minds of American citizens than a flood of official press releases. First, there was the comment as he was wheeled into surgery after being shot by a would-be assassin. To the doctors about to perform surgery, the president quipped, "I hope you're all Republicans."

A few years later in the debates with presidential contender Walter Mondale, seventy-three-year-old Reagan was questioned about his age and his ability to lead the nation in a second term: "I will not make age an issue in this campaign. I am not going to exploit for political reasons my opponent's youth and inexperience."

Humor also serves its purpose when it permits us to be children again, to step outside the adult role of always having the answers and handling the problems correctly, and the pressure that comes with that role. We can laugh for a few minutes and postpone the tears involved in solving a problem. A family was called into the office of the school superintendent to discuss what should be done about their son, who had been caught selling marijuana to his schoolmates. Although he had a broken heart and every intention of doing whatever it took to solve the problem, the father was able to step out of his adult role as problem solver for a brief moment through his sense of humor: "Well, obviously this kid's a born salesman; all we've got to do is find him a better product."

Humor can be a powerful tension reliever, especially the kind of humor that brings a belly laugh. When people with potential conflicts are thrown into a situation together, a joking relationship often permits them to relax in an environment where everyone agrees not to take offense.

During former President Bush's trip to Japan to discuss controversial trade agreements, he came down with a bad case of the flu and passed out at a state dinner. When he regained consciousness, he quipped to the frightened hosts at his side, "Why don't you just let me lie here and sleep it off?" The tension and potential embarrassment of the situation began to melt immediately.

Another benefit of humor is that it creates a bond between people. When two people allude to something with a knowing wink and smile, informing other listeners, "That's an old joke," they draw a circle around themselves. "We've been through the fire together," they say, "and we've shuffled something into a solution, or at least into perspective." Humor often brings people into emotional intimacy.

Self-deprecating humor can help us rise above feelings of inferiority. A popular notion says if we can laugh at ourselves before others do, we're well-adjusted people. A speaker at a large industry gathering began his speech: "My mother would laugh at the irony of this situation — a 'C' chemistry student standing to address a roomful of Ph.D. chemists. . . . There has to be some justice in this." From then on, he had the audience in the palm of his hand as he explained that perhaps his role in speaking to such a well-educated audience was simply to share a different perspective on a common problem.

With such self-deprecating humor, we disarm our potential critics and cast a protective shell around our shoulders, lessening the effect of any forthcoming criticism.

Even physical benefits can result from a good strong laugh. Laughter can relieve headaches and lower blood pressure. On some of the TV commercials with before and after headache sufferers, I often wonder if the cured person's smile came before or after the headache left. Which was the cause and which the effect? Sometimes it would be cheaper and quicker to listen to a child's laughter than to reach into the medicine cabinet.

Finally, our sense of humor attracts others to God. Seventeenth-century Protestant clergyman James Usher observed, "If good people would but make their goodness agreeable and smile instead of frowning in their virtue, how many would they win to the good cause?" A good sense of humor may be the most important thing to wear when you go out in public.

But for all the positive attractions of humor, we should be wary of its ambiguous nature.

Some people use it to probe another's values and interests when they're not sure how the listener feels. For example, if someone tells a racist or lewd joke and the listener joins in the laughter, the joke-teller assumes the listener shares his devaluation of women, sex, or an entire race. If the listener doesn't respond to the would-be humor, the teller knows he's on dangerous ground and can back down without an outright declaration of his attitudes or values.

Many political analysts believe that Clayton Williams lost the Texas governor's race to Ann Richards because of his joke about women "enjoying" rape. What he thought funny revealed an offensive value system.

As far as our Christian witness goes, what we *don't* laugh at may be as important as what we *do* laugh at. English author Izaak Walton had the right perspective when he said, "I love such mirth as does not make friends ashamed to look upon one another next morning."

But we should also pay close attention to the last portion of Proverbs 17:22: "a broken spirit dries the bones."

Humor should spread a smile, but not wrinkle a brow. We may use self-deprecating wit on ourselves as a shield of self-defense, but we should never use sarcasm as a sword to wound others. It was fitting that H. Ross Perot wittily punned, "I'm all ears," during the 1992 presidential debates. Had the comment come from his challengers, they would have been pegged boorish.

We've often heard the cliché "Your freedom to swing your arm ends where my nose begins." Where humor is concerned, your freedom to benefit from humor ends where another's broken spirit begins. Many an adult can still recall the pain of being laughed at as a child.

Who gets the brunt of humor aimed at others? Sociologist Rose Laub Coser did a study of the uses of humor among the staff of a mental hospital. She found that humor almost always flows downward; that is, those higher up in the organizational hierarchy make jokes at the expense of those workers beneath them. Office humor may be our way of supporting the social structure; we laugh at others' expense because we want to feel superior. But whether inflicted out of a need to make ourselves feel better or out of sheer insensitivity, wounds created by humor at someone else's expense go deep.

Does all this mean that we should check our sense of humor at the office door? Of course not.

There are those of us who laugh too much and those who laugh too little. We can use our sense of humor to attract others to our faith or to repel them with our reserve and pride. The idea is to be as free — and as careful — with how we use our humor as how we use our checkbook.

For Further Reflection:

> Singing to someone in deep sorrow
> is like pouring vinegar in an open cut. (Prov. 25:20 CEV)

> Sorrow may hide behind laughter,
> and happiness may end in sorrow. (Prov. 14:13 CEV)

Failure — and Not Yet Forty

My heart throbs, my strength fails me;
as for the light of my eyes — it also has gone from me.
My friends and companions stand aloof from my affliction,
and my neighbors stand far off.

(Ps. 38:10–11 NRSV)

Answer me speedily, O LORD;
My spirit fails!
Do not hide Your face from me,
Lest I be like those who go down into the pit.
Cause me to hear Your lovingkindness in the morning,
For in You do I trust;
Cause me to know the way in which I should walk,
For I lift up my soul to You.

(Ps. 143:7–8)

Arnold Schwarzenegger's income per movie has reached $15 million. Madonna closed a deal for $60 million over the next seven years. The average salary for major league baseball players topped $1 million in 1992. The President's annual salary is $200,000. The average teacher makes $34,413 a year. The pope has no salary at all.

Although many give lip service to the idea that success can't be measured in dollars and cents, in the business world one seems to be evidence of the other. That is, income — or the lack of it — is often the yardstick for success or failure.

Rare is the employee who has never compared his or her bank account to that of another individual: "If I'd been as sharp as Joe, I'd have developed that idea and started a business like his." Or, "If I'd finished that degree, I'd be a little more eager to go to that class reunion."

We may agree wholeheartedly that money doesn't necessarily equal success, but most of us nevertheless feel like failures from time to time. We forget that success is not external; it's internal.

If it's not the size of our paycheck that brings on that gnawing desperation, it may be continual put-downs from the boss. It may be a failure in marriage or in other family relationships or friendships. It may be failure in overcoming a personal habit. It may be failure caused by poor health. Whatever the reason, let's consider the feeling of failure more closely.

Proverbs 14:23 tells us that in all work (even failure) there is profit. If you've ever spent $50,000 manufacturing a product nobody wants to buy, you know that verse has to be referring to something other than financial profit!

So what's the profit? With the right thought process, we can psychologically prepare not to repeat our failures. For example, physiologist Robert Pozos of the University of Minnesota in Duluth has shown that a person who falls into frigid water but remains calm will suffer a slower drop in core temperature than one who panics.

Studies by Niels Birbaumer of Pennsylvania State University have shown that patients can even raise the temperature of their hands and feet by using mental imagery, such as imagining they are touching hot coals. Birbaumer notes that apparently the part of the brain that controls higher thought can actually change physical activity.

If we as humans can think ourselves out of freezing to death, surely we can think ourselves out of failure! Failure can be profit. It teaches us the following lessons:

We Can't Please Everyone

Comedian Bill Cosby says, "I don't know the key to success, but the key to failure is trying to please everybody." Many people wake up in mid-life to find that they have spent all their energy trying to please a spouse, a parent, a friend, or a boss. Job certainly knew what it was to stand against what family and friends told him was wrong with his life. Listening to them was like listening to a daily litany of failure.

The American wife and mother has been facing this dilemma for the last two decades. Women who work outside the home look down on those who've chosen to stay at home and think of them as unmotivated, uninteresting, and uninterested in the world around them. At the other extreme are those stay-at-home women who make those who've chosen to work outside the home feel like failures as mothers. Neither group wins when they try to set the guidelines for each others' lives.

We rarely feel successful when we let those around us put their thumbs on our measuring scale. Remember that God will be the final judge of how we spend our days.

We Learn to Take Risks

Around the jogging track, we comfort each other with "No pain, no gain." In the corporate world, it's "No risks, no payback." We have to invest money, time, and effort in most projects to make them pay off.

When I was confronted with more business than I could handle alone, I faced my first real risk. Do I make clients wait by having them book workshop dates far into the future? Or, do I risk an associate's salary, invest the time to train him or her, and hope the profits warrant the additional staff? Then the second risk: Do I move out of my home office into larger office space? Risk after risk through the years. But with risk comes reward.

Look at your failure and ask: What was I not willing to risk? The time for proper education before jumping? The money to do the proper research? The effort to be persuasive?

Just as an empty stall stays clean, an unexercised muscle doesn't get a cramp. But neither does it perform at its best. If you never take risks, you probably won't make a mistake, but neither will you enjoy the feeling of success.

Learn to think of risks as investments in your future. If all you have to show for your life so far is a clean stable or failure, then act.

We Learn to Follow God's Laws

God is a God of order, the Bible tells us, and that order often includes the causes and effects of our failures.

If we are talking about financial failure, we may have not heeded God's warning that the wise man cheerfully gives. If we're talking about failure as a Christian businessperson standing against immorality, we may not have studied the Word of God and taken its principles seriously enough to make the tough but morally right decisions.

Sooner or later any successful person will be tested on honesty. Our first test came when a client paid us $12,000 in advance for training classes to be conducted in the coming year. The training director wanted to pay us from her end-of-the-year budget and forwarded a check to cover classes we were to conduct the following February. Those classes were postponed until May. And then moved to August. The training director then left the job without word to us or any direction about what to do with the $12,000. We found out she'd left only after we tried to reach her and got her assistant. The assistant promised to check into the situation and let us know the status of the project. Within months, the assistant also left the company.

Result? We were left holding $12,000 for unper-formed work that no one at the client's organization seemed to know anything about—or care about, for that matter. Finally, after much effort on our part, we were able to return the money to the client with our explanation about what had happened. Without that effort, we would have been $12,000 richer and nobody would have been the wiser.

Except God. Tests are tests. Laws are laws.

We Become Aware of Our Own Strengths and Weaknesses

Although almost everyone does it from time to time, placing blame is seldom appropriate or fully accurate. We learn to quit blaming our family for "holding us back," our boss for "unclear directions," and our colleagues for not "warning us about what was ahead."

Researchers at the Center for Creative Leadership in Greensboro, North Carolina, asked seventy-six highly successful women in major corporations if they had ever failed on the job and taken a career misstep. Nearly three-quarters of the respondents reported at least one major setback. The most frequently mentioned failures were the failure to sell one's ideas in the company and the failure to carry through on ideas or assigned projects. Yet all these prominent, successful women ultimately succeeded because they pinpointed their *own* weaknesses and went to work on correcting those trouble spots.

We Learn to Overcome Shame

Since childhood, we have been programmed to consider, "What will they think of me?" If you act ashamed and defeated, people will treat you that way.

In 1963, fresh out of college, Lionel Aldridge began his life as a pro football player with the Green Bay Packers and, as a part of that team, won three straight National Football League championships and the first two Super Bowls. His coach, Vince Lombardi, made a lasting impression on him as he talked of success not in terms of never falling down but in always getting up after a fall.

Due to a chemical imbalance, Lionel became schizophrenic. For years he refused the medication that would correct the problem because he was ashamed of the side effects: impotence, protruding tongue, stiffened arms and legs. For seven years he heard voices and could not function. He lost his family, his job, and his friends as a result. After he admitted his powerlessness to help himself, he sought medical treatment and was cured. No longer ashamed, he now speaks to groups about his mental illness and recovery in an effort to dispel despair caused by failure.

Companies fail, politicians fail, sports figures fail. Someone has said that failure is not contagious unless you act as though you are a carrier.

We Learn to Cope with Disappointment

There is nothing new about despair and depression. The psalmist David, the prophet Jonah, and the long-suffering Job were the most notably depressed writers in the Bible. Undoubtedly, at times the apostle Paul, too, felt disappointed at being locked up in a prison cell rather than preaching on a street corner. He must have also felt irritation at having to defend himself against false teachers and having to "prove" he was dedicated to the cause of the gospel.

People throughout history have experienced a sense of depression and failure; Winston Churchill called it his "black dog." And Abraham Lincoln was no stranger to the feeling. Someone once summed up his road to the White House like this: Failed in business in 1831. Defeated for legislature in 1832. Second failure in business in 1833. Suffered nervous breakdown in 1836. Defeated for House Speaker in 1838. Defeated for elector in 1840. Defeated for Congress in 1843. Defeated for Congress in 1848. Defeated for Senate in 1855. Defeated for vice president in 1856. Defeated for Senate in 1858. Elected president in 1860.

Alexander Graham Bell was unable to sell his telephone to Western Union. Chester Carlson's idea of xerographic copying was rejected by several major corporations before it sparked the growth of Xerox Corporation. Computers originally left Tom Watson, head of IBM, "nonplussed" about their usefulness, and he reportedly estimated the world market for them to be about five buyers.

A survey by Dun and Bradstreet Corporation revealed that 60,432 businesses failed in the United States in 1990. The trend continued in 1991 and 1992. Others may be wrong in the way they react to our ideas and efforts, but today's failures may be tomorrow's biggest success stories. In the meantime, disappointment is part of the process. Disappointment is a part of the human condition that helps highlight times of satisfaction for a job well done.

We Accept Our Inability to Control the World

Oh, sure, we all know that, in theory; it's only in practice that things get fuzzy. We can't control our health. We can't control our subordinates and make them want to do a good job. We can't control our bosses and make them give us the right decisions. We can't control industry flukes or the whims of the American consumer. Who would have ever guessed telegrams and record players would have come and gone so quickly?

Yet some businesspeople, through a series of successes that they have erroneously chalked up to their own efforts rather than to God's graciousness, begin to feel invincible. It often takes the unpredictable to make us recognize God's control in our lives.

We Find a New, More Worthy Goal

We may find new friends who have been through the same experiences and can encourage us. A change of activities can give us a totally new perspective.

Vincent van Gogh made that discovery with a change of goals. He came to his art in only the last ten years of his life, having tried and failed at selling art and school teaching, and at preaching, where the evangelical authorities dismissed him for his "excessive" zeal in helping Belgian coal miners. His brother supported him all his life because he sold only one picture for five francs. In the last three months of his life, Van Gogh was still experimenting, striving toward his ideal; he painted twelve pictures in a new format, the double square. After life-long bouts with mental illness and despair over his "failures," he took his own life. In 1990, his painting *Portrait du Dr. Gachet* sold for a staggering $82.5 million.

We Learn to Overcome Fear

God alone—not money or bosses or new ideas or our own expertise or hard work—controls our destiny. Perfect trust and love of Him casts out fear.

Failure is only failure when we fail to learn from our experiences.

For Further Reflection:

If you faint in the day of adversity, your strength ... [is] small. (Prov. 24:10 NRSV)

In all toil there is profit, but mere talk leads only to poverty. (Prov. 14:23 NRSV)

He who covers his sins will not prosper,
But whoever confesses and forsakes them will have mercy. (Prov. 28:13)

Trust in the LORD with all your heart,
And lean not on your own understanding;
In all your ways acknowledge Him,
And He shall direct your paths. (Prov. 3:5–6)

And now I am about to go the way of all the earth, and you know in your hearts and souls, all of you, that not one thing has failed of all the good things that the Lord your God promised concerning you; all have come to pass for you, not one of them has failed. (Josh. 23:14 NRSV)

Be strong and of good courage, do not fear nor be afraid of them; for the Lord your God, He is the One who goes with you. He will not leave you nor forsake you. (Deut. 31:6)

Be Ye Kind to Your Customers

And just as you want men to do to you,
you also do to them likewise.
(Luke 6:31)

And the King will answer and say to them,
"Assuredly, I say to you, inasmuch as you did it
to one of the least of these My brethren,
you did it to Me. . . ." Then He will answer them, saying,
"Assuredly, I say to you, inasmuch as you did not do it
to one of the least of these, you did not do it to Me."
(Matt. 25:40, 45)

Like the proverbial average family that moves every five years, we get the itch to mow a new lawn. Finding the house of our dreams, we apply for a loan with Mortgage Company X, which guarantees in-house approval within thirty to forty-five days. "Will I need a CPA-prepared financial worth statement since I'm self-employed?" I ask. "If so, I want to get it now rather than slow up the process somewhere down the line."

"No problem," the loan officer answers. "If you keep your own books, your statement is good enough."

A few days later, the loan officer calls to say she has lost the VA eligibility certificate. Can we supply another? We do. A few days after that, she phones to say that they do, after all, need our CPA to prepare a statement. He does. We wait.

Finally approval comes. But two hours before closing, our realtor calls to say there will be no closing. Mortgage Company X does not intend to honor the "VA point" commitment they made at the time of application. Somehow the loan officer had never gotten around to putting it in writing for us. What's more, the loan officer in charge of our file has been fired.

After a conversation with our lawyer, who merely shakes his head, we drop by to see the person in charge at Mortgage Company X. A receptionist is holding down the fort; the head office has decided "to relieve from duty" all loan officers at that location, and others will be flying in shortly from headquarters to hear our complaints. A couple of days later they "permit" us to quietly take our loan package to another institution. We run.

But that is just the beginning. After signing on the dotted line with Mortgage Company Y, we breathe a sigh of gratitude and pull out the home-furnishings catalogs. Custom window coverings come from Department Store A. The master bedroom woven-wood window covering is two inches too short and two inches too narrow. Would I mind if they just spray on a chemical treatment and "yank" it down? I say okay. They do. It doesn't work. They refund the money, and I'm "only out" the four-week delay.

I call Store B. Humming at the typewriter while the installer hangs the second window covering, I dream of privacy in the bedroom. But the installer comes down the hall shaking his head. "You wanted a double-pull wood, ma'am? I'm afraid the factory made a mistake. I'm going to have to send this back."

On Store B's second delivery, I'm afraid to look. "Ma'am," the installer says, "you're not going to believe this, but they made the same mistake. It's the same one we sent back." I get the correct window covering six weeks later.

Store C delivers a brass bed for my daughter's room. One hole for the frame is drilled higher than the other. "But it is a $34 special," the salesclerk reminds me on the phone. My husband drills a lower hole.

The master bedroom brass headboard, a more expensive variety, we don't dare leave for a delivery truck. The salesman will send it to package pickup while we pull the car around. He does and we do. In the bedroom light, after we've unloaded the headboard with (literally) gloved hands, we see the scratches — headboard to footboard. Yes, the salesman says on the phone, we can return it if we bring it back immediately. He "had a feeling" package pickup would be careless with it. "They do it all the time," he assures us. It is the only headboard of its kind in stock.

The following Saturday, Store D delivers the new washer; the old one, in its twelfth year, had washed its last load a week earlier. During the new washer's test spin cycle, a smoky scent fills the house. The repairman says its motor can't possibly be burned out. It is.

After only two tries, Store E delivers the fireplace screen (without the screws) and a dinette. It seems they delivered both to the old billing address rather than the one we had carefully printed on the contract under "Deliver To." "Be glad to give you a refund on the fireplace screen if you want to bring it back," the clerk says. Is it worth the forty-five-minute trip across town? We find the screws to fit at the corner hardware store and make do.

The garage-door opener we buy as an unassembled do-it-yourself kit. After installation, the remote controls don't control. The store owner promises to have the manufacturer send new ones. They come ten days later, C.O.D. for $62. After refusing the delivery, we phone the store again. Ownership has changed hands, and the owner "doesn't know" about honoring the old guarantee. *Old* guarantee? Eleven days? My husband takes the opener off the garage door and returns it anyway. How can they refuse eyeball to eyeball? They do.

"If you'll come back tomorrow, when the repairman is around to be sure you didn't damage the controls when you installed it, we'll see about a replacement," the new owner says. After the second forty-five-minute trip the following day, the repairman verifies that the remote controls never controlled. Our refund is uncheerfully given.

Have we been singled out for this persecution, we wonder. Is the rest of the world faring any better? Not even our daily newspaper will tell us; the paper deliveryman argues that our street is nonexistent. Four days and two lengthy direction sessions later, we get a paper.

So much for the outside world. But can we make contact? I've always been one to get mail. The second week after our move, our mail dwindles to "Dear Occupant" circulars. A trip to our old address produces approximately an eight-inch stack of first-class mail.

Yes, the postal supervisor says, they do still have the change-of-address notice on file. But they frequently have a sub on the route, and possibly nobody has told him to forward the mail. The supervisor will "take care of it personally." Four months and numerous phone calls later, we resort to removing the mailbox from the pole at our old address. They can't leave it there without a box, can they?

Anticipating such "disruptions of service," we had planned early phone installation. One month before M-Day, I call to have telephone service transferred and to ask for a cost estimate. A "marketing specialist" will have to call me back because my order is "complicated." After hearing nothing for two weeks, I phone again. The representative apologizes for the delay and promises to give the order "her personal attention." I ask if she can give me an assigned number; she does, insisting, of course, that the number can't be guaranteed until installation. I understand. Relying on the "96 percent chance" that the number will work, I use the number in a national ad. The next day, the representative calls back to explain that she made a mistake in assigning the number and figuring the charges.

Four weeks later, the installer phones me. He wants to know where I am. He's at the new residence to install the phone and the house is empty. I tell him about the rescheduling due to Mortgage Company X's shenanigans, and give him the contact name, date, and hour of rescheduling. He never got the word, he says. We reschedule for a week later.

I wait in a cold, empty house for the installer to arrive between 8:00 A.M. and 5:00 P.M. At 4:55, he shows up. The phone works, but the answering service will take another five days. Thank goodness for at least one inefficiency; they have failed to put the transfer tape on the old number. The outside world can still contact me.

Fifty-four days after my original order request I have a working telephone. Rejoicing, I phone friends with the correct new number. But when I try to dial the downtown library, I can't. Have they done what I think they have? Yes. The operator verifies that they have installed a limited suburban line instead of the metro service I ordered.

Two days later, the bill arrives for one month's service. Since the phone has been working for only forty-six hours, I call to complain. "Not to worry," the representative tells me. She will adjust the bill and send a corrected copy.

A disruption-of-service notice arrives. I phone to say that I have never received a corrected bill. "We'll make a note not to disconnect, then," the representative says, "so don't worry." I do.

Two days later, the phone isn't working; my line is crossed with another number. They correct the problem twelve days later.

Customer Relations calls to ask about "the manner in which my recent order has been handled." Is it worth fifteen minutes to tell her? I decide it is, giving her names and dates. "This is my job," she gushes, "to catch problems like this. I'm going to give this to my supervisor for his personal attention, and he'll get back to you."

No one ever calls back from Customer Relations.

We all have our own stories to tell, from an automobile with defective tires to chocolate-chip cupcakes with no chips from the supermarket bakery.

Has it always been so? Not necessarily. James Cash Penney, starting in 1902, built a multibillion-dollar business empire on the Golden Rule principle. In fact, for years his stores were called The Golden Rule Stores and operated on the principle of treating customers as the owner himself wanted to be treated.

Employees and their employers in the 1990s have certainly been alerted to the decline of customer service and satisfaction. According to a study conducted for the American Society for Quality Control, 41 percent of corporate executives surveyed said that quality control will be the most critical business issue in the coming years. In fact, 57 percent said that improving product quality will be more important than increasing profits or reducing costs.

Disregard for the customer cannot be blamed on the lack of modern-day prophets. W. Edwards Deming and Joseph Juran, who share the reputation for saving Japan's economy after the war, have long preached their message of high quality in product development and manufacturing. To paraphrase Juran, American business operates on a policy of "take the money and run" rather than meeting the needs of customers over the lifetime of the product or service.

The Malcolm Baldrige Award, presented annually to companies for their quality efforts, evidences a reawakening to the importance of excellent workmanship and service. Many have put their finger directly on the hurt. But has American business listened?

When the average department hears that the CEO is coming for a visit, they spit and polish their operation until service shines. Do they not understand that God's visits come more regularly?

Look around your office. Would you want to be your own customer and pay for the service and product you sell? Does a friend or family member get better service from you than your "average" customer? Would you sell the same products to the Lord, or would you advise Him to shop elsewhere for quality? Would your services be rendered more timely, carefully, or cheerfully if He were your customer? If you've done it (or not done it) to the least of these my brethren . . .

For Further Reflection:

Let each of you look not to your own interests, but to the interests of others. (Phil. 2:4 NRSV)

Respect for Authority: Rendering unto Caesar and Mrs. Jones

Remind them to be subject to rulers and authorities,
to be obedient, to be ready for every good work.
(Titus 3:1 NRSV)

Let every person be subject to the governing authorities;
for there is no authority except from God, and
those authorities that exist have been instituted by God.
Therefore whoever resists authority resists what
God has appointed, and those who resist will incur
judgment.... For the same reason you also pay taxes,
for the authorities are God's servants, busy
with this very thing. Pay to all what is due them — taxes
to whom taxes are due, revenue to whom revenue is due,
respect to whom respect is due, honor to whom honor is due.
(Rom. 13:1-2, 6-7 NRSV)

And Jesus answered and said to them, "Render to Caesar
the things that are Caesar's, and to God the things
that are God's." And they marveled at Him.
(Mark 12:17)

"What you hide from the tax man can put you into beachfront property," a New York City Department of Finance ad promised several years ago. But what the ad referred to by way of beachfront property was Rikers Island, the New Yorker's Alcatraz. Other ads try to humor the tax dodger. One such ad featured a man in his home cheating on his income tax return. Then the scene fades to a penitentiary, where the same man sits behind bars with a file. The caption said, "You can file now, or you can file later."

Publicity campaigns to lure tax cheaters to pay up have become a last resort for many state and local governments suffering from the actions of those individual citizens who have decided to buck the taxing authority and write their own laws and loopholes.

Probably nowhere is our will to submit to authority in government tested more stridently than in the area of taxes.

How serious is the problem? According to IRS estimates, 17 percent of our taxpayers do not comply with the tax laws. The result is a gross tax underpayment that amounted to $100 billion in 1991. If taxpayers paid all the taxes they legally owe, we could wipe out the national debt in a few short years. And that $100 billion a year estimate does not include the tens of billions not paid by drug czars and other criminals (*Money*, April 1991).

According to a study by the market research firm of Yankelovich, Skelly and White, Inc., one out of five citizens admits to some form of tax cheating; one in three thinks such behavior is expected and acceptable.

Do the ad campaigns work? Former Minnesota revenue commissioner Tom Riplette, quoted in a *Newsweek* interview several years ago, estimated that every dollar spent on enforcement publicity can yield between six and seven dollars in recovered revenue.

But is it conscience that brings the cheaters around? No, government officials insist, it's simply the humiliation of public exposure. In other words, they care more about what men think of their cheating than what God thinks.

A small business owner recently confessed such a weakness— of which God alone had convicted him and for which he intended to make restitution. The business owner commented on the temptation he faced not to show all his income on his books and to add personal expenses to the corporate accounts. He came to the conclusion that these bookkeeping tactics were nothing less than stealing from the government and defying God-ordained authority.

That realization and turnaround comes almost exclusively with the understanding that our obedience to authority is by God's command.

But perhaps the authority even closer to many of us than the corporate tax books is the authority of our immediate supervisor on the job. The manager strides in and interrupts, "I need these reports by five tonight, and you need to cancel all further projects and out-of-town travel until further notice."

"Who says?" a chorus of voices asks.

Sound familiar? People are still asking about the authority of those who give orders just as the people in Jesus' day continually asked him: "By what authority are you doing these things?" (Matthew 21:23).

Human nature has always defied authority. It was that same proud attitude that caused Satan to be cast from heaven and resulted in the fall of man.

"High office is like a pyramid," says French philosopher d'Alembert. "Only two kinds of animals reach the summit, reptiles and eagles." We, as employees, prefer to be on an eagle's team and to defy, thwart, and bring down the reptiles.

But when Jesus said, "Blessed are the meek," He did not make the statement conditional on the personality of the one we must respect and defer to. Meekness is not weakness; it's willful submission.

Thoreau insisted, in his *Civil Disobedience*, "That government is best which governs least." Most businesspeople would agree, especially when Congress is about to pass legislation that directly affects their industry.

But the only biblical permission we have to disobey authority occurs where that authority directly defies God's laws. "We ought to obey God rather than men" (Acts 5:29). However, most of our disrespect and defiance of authority is not the result of being commanded to do something dishonest or immoral on the job. Rather, our disrespect usually stems from self-interest: our dislike of an individual or an assigned task.

The issue may be as small as refusing to show up to work on time. Have you ever totaled up the cost of lost productivity of 500 employees who show up to work only five minutes late two mornings a week? Staggering. If their authority figure doesn't threaten to dismiss them, they shrug off the issue. Disrespect.

Or there's the matter of participative management. When managers invite team members to discuss a situation and express an opinion and then make a decision contrary to the wishes of one member of the group, the result is often sabotage of the project by the disgruntled employee. That employee has confused disagreement with disrespect.

If employers could not count on respect for authority, our businesses would have little to distinguish them from cattle herds or amusement park crowds. Respect for authority is an act and attitude of humility, self-denial, care of the common good of our business and society, and faith in God's providence.

Submission to authority is victory over our uncivilized nature.

For Further Reflection:

> For rebellion is as the sin of witchcraft,
> And stubbornness is as iniquity and idolatry. (1 Sam. 15:23)

> Obey those who rule over you, and be submissive, for they watch out for your souls, as those who must give account. Let them do so with joy and not with grief, for that would be unprofitable for you. (Heb. 13:17)

> Slaves, you must always obey your earthly masters. Try to please them at all times, and not just when you think they are watching. Honor the Lord and serve your masters with your whole heart. Do your work willingly, as though you were serving the Lord himself, and not just your earthly master. In fact, the Lord Christ is the one you are really serving, and you know that he will reward you. (Col. 3:22–24 CEV)

How God Reads the Bottom Line

The LORD doesn't like it
when we cheat in business.
Justice makes rulers powerful.
They should hate evil.
(Prov. 16:11–12 CEV)

The integrity of the upright will guide them,
But the perversity of the unfaithful will destroy them.
(Prov. 11:3)

Every way of a man is right in his own eyes,
But the LORD weighs the hearts.
(Prov. 21:2)

Better is a little with righteousness,
Than vast revenues without justice.
(Prov. 16:8)

We have a new corporate function floating around now — ethics consultant. Insider trading scandals have focused a spotlight on Congress and Wall Street and made executives all over the country take note of "right" again. Specifically, former Securities and Exchange Commission Chairman John Shad gave Harvard Business School $20 million to establish a program in ethics.

That's good, because for the past few years, we've been throwing around the term *situational ethics* as if there were such a thing. By definition, ethics is an absolute standard of right and wrong — morality versus immorality. If it's situational, it's not ethics.

We have problems determining what is and what is not a quality product or service. Every year we see the concerned media publish lists of unsafe toys to avoid for Christmas gifts, of unhealthy foods, of harmful cosmetics, or dangerous medicines.

We have problems determining appropriate wages for employees, yet Luke 10:7 and James 5:4 tell us that a laborer is worthy of adequate, honest wages.

We keep lawyers busy handling cases where our word is not our bond. We keep ourselves covered in our own paperwork because no one trusts oral directions, directives, or confirmations. Several years ago, I did a survey of fourteen client organizations to ask about their paperwork habits and productivity. One question asked: "What is the most frequent unnecessary document written in your company?" The overwhelming response? Memos and reports to cover themselves. In other words, people put things in writing simply so that if something goes wrong they can say, "It's not my fault."

We have problems with people taking advantage of the little guy. Someone has said that there is much more thievery going on in front of the customer counter than behind it. Big companies often take advantage of their small suppliers by asking for bigger and bigger volume discounts, threatening to take their business elsewhere.

For suppliers and vendors who depend on a few large customers, this tactic almost always works. The alternative is simply to close the front door and turn out the light.

We have problems with people claiming credit for work they didn't do and facts they don't have. Carl King, president of Team Building Systems, an employee screener in Houston, says thirty percent of all resumes are falsified (*Inc.*, August 1992).

When was the last time you compared a resume submitted in response to a job to the real job described by that applicant's supervisor? We do so routinely, and we're amazed at the exaggerations and gross misrepresentations recorded on resumes.

And the scientific community is not immune from equally flagrant deceptions. "False Prophets," a publication by Alexander Kohn of Tel Aviv Medical School, explores the reasons behind fraud among scientists. A well-publicized fraud at Harvard Medical School involved the testing of heart drugs on dogs. Other such examples abound. In a publish-or-perish environment, many have evidently chosen to publish and pray no one verifies.

We have problems with bribes and payoffs. The National Collegiate Athletic Association repeatedly blows the whistle on coaches, administrators, boards of directors, and booster clubs that tuck improper payments into the hands of amateur players for clothes, cars, and carousing. School officials who try to squelch the practices often lose their jobs.

We have problems with corporate stealing. Video and audio companies offering free previews of their materials frequently catch potential customers illegally copying or sharing their tapes. And some thieves are so blatant as to photograph their competitors' product designs at trade shows and then go back to their own drawing board to duplicate the designs.

Electronic eavesdroppers repeatedly underbid their competition by very slim margins and seem to be always one step ahead on marketing strategies and advertising campaigns. In fact, this problem is so prevalent that businesses are advised to keep the main telephone secured and to ask all service technicians for identification.

Further, they are advised not to place telephones, tape recorders, or any electronic devices in rooms where confidential discussions are conducted. If those precautions don't curtail the stealing, they routinely have "debugging sweeps," including radio frequency analysis and physical searches performed by a security firm.

As global competition grows, according to Peter Schweizer, author of *Friendly Spies*, business intelligence will become a major priority. He says, "Business secrets have become more vital than military secrets."

So what can be done about the "situational ethics" problem?

Employee training has been touted as the answer to a multitude of problems in the workplace, and the chaos created by a floating ethical standard has been no exception. Executives are calling in consultants and house trainers to give crash courses on right and wrong.

But I'm of the opinion that by the time the individual gets to the marketplace, his or her ethical mindset is fairly well coded. Little — short of conversion and God's conviction — can change that inner code from "The end justifies the means" to "The methods forecast the end."

And that change of conscience as an individual employee may cost your job. Such was the case with William B. Walton, one of the cofounders of the Holiday Inn chain. In his book *The New Bottom Line*, he says he resigned because the company's policies departed from the founders' evangelical religious principles.

Playing the part of the corporate conscience as a whistle-blower can be even more dangerous. Such was the case of New York City police officer Frank Serpico, who uncovered graft in his own police force. When his efforts to clean up the corruption from within failed, he opted for the front page of *The New York Times*. He was shot.

If you haven't come to a decision or test, consider what's at stake when you violate God's clear-cut principles of conducting business. In the final pay period, whose payroll do you want to be on?

For Further Reflection:

Our inner thoughts are a lamp from the LORD,
and they search our hearts.
Rulers are protected by God's mercy and loyalty,
but they must be merciful for their kingdoms to last.
(Prov. 20:27–28 CEV)

All things are lawful for me, but not all things are helpful; all things are lawful for me, but not all things edify. (1 Cor. 10:23)

Abstain from every form of evil. (1 Thess. 5:22)

Pray for us; for we are confident that we have a good conscience, in all things desiring to live honorably. (Heb. 13:18)

We have renounced the shameful things that one hides; we refuse to practice cunning or to falsify God's word; but by the open statement of the truth we commend ourselves to the conscience of everyone in the sight of God. (2 Cor. 4:2 NRSV)

For we intend to do what is right not only in the Lord's sight but also in the sight of others. (2 Cor. 8:21 NRSV)

I refuse to be corrupt
or to take part
in anything crooked. (Ps. 101:3 CEV)

Listen! The wages of the laborers who mowed your fields, which you kept back by fraud, cry out, and the cries of the harvesters have reached the ears of the Lord of hosts. (James 5:4 NRSV)

Treasures of wickedness profit nothing,
But righteousness delivers from death. (Prov. 10:2)

To do righteousness and justice
Is more acceptable to the LORD than sacrifice.
(Prov. 21:3)

One who increases his possessions by usury and extortion
Gathers it for him who will pity the poor. (Prov. 28:8)

Two things the LORD hates
are dishonest scales
and dishonest measures.
The good or bad
that children do
shows what they are like. (Prov. 20:10–11 CEV)

Bread gained by deceit is sweet to a man,
But afterward his mouth will be filled with gravel.
(Prov. 20:17)

He who works deceit shall not dwell within my house;
He who tells lies shall not continue in my presence.
(Ps. 101:7)

Happy are those who observe justice,
who do righteousness at all times. (Ps. 106:3 NRSV)

Stealing Your Shirt and Computer Database

You shall not steal.
(Ex. 20:15)

Cheating to get rich is a foolish dream
and no less than suicide.
(Prov. 21:6 CEV)

Retail stores call it *inventory shrinkage*. Supermarkets refer to it as *spoilage*. If we throw away the euphemisms, we're talking about theft. The United States Chamber of Commerce says theft on the job costs U.S. businesses $40 billion annually.

Often, the corporate culprits are the employees themselves! Ron Zemke, in an article for *Training* magazine (May 1986) cites a study of retail businesses done by Arthur Young, an international accounting and consulting firm, that says merchants assigned 43 percent of their losses from theft to employees and only 30 percent to shoplifters.

Employees themselves admit their guilt. Stanton Corporation, a North Carolina firm specializing in theft prevention in the workplace, reports that in a survey of 7,000 retail job applicants, 30 percent admitted to stealing at least $10 worth of merchandise from a former employer. The average "take" of these employees was $33.97.

But before we as Christian readers smugly plead not guilty, we should think again—on matters other than pilfering cash. Let me mention a few thefts I've heard about recently: A friend in my Bible study class asked for prayer about what to do in a situation where his colleague is stealing copies of all the software from his employer and selling it on the side. Another acquaintance waits to call her relatives from her work phone over the weekend because no one notices the charges.

And the theft of trade secrets is a temptation in corporations of all sizes. Newspapers frequently report lawsuits over higher-ups in companies taking trade secrets for new products or services to a competitor. In fact, the biggest concern in small consulting businesses such as mine is hiring employees who learn the materials and methods and then set themselves up in business using that information.

Even pastors are not immune to the temptation to get "something for nothing." A friend of mine who runs a nursery was appalled by his pastor, who recently stole several hundred dollars of plants and labor from him. Oh, I'm sure the pastor didn't see it that way. You see, the pastor had just accepted the new pastorate and moved into the neighborhood, and asked the church-member owner of the nursery to come help him with his landscaping. After the landscaper finished the work and presented him with the bill, the pastor acted astonished and said he couldn't afford to pay. He had expected the nursery owner to do the work without charge.

Is employee theft a relatively new concern? Well, not new, exactly, but it's certainly on the increase. In a study done in the early 1960s, similar to the 1986 study I mentioned earlier, only 12 percent of the employees admitted stealing from an employer. Likewise, a newspaper distributor laments the change he's seen in how newspapers have been sold during the last twenty years. Twenty years ago, they had "honor racks" where patrons simply dropped in their coins and lifted the rack for their papers. Today the biggest problem he has with his 120 newspaper machines is vandalism — toothpicks and slugs shoved in the coin slots to get the papers without paying. Twenty years ago, the JCPenney company did not even prosecute for employee theft; today they keep the shrinkage problem in front of their employees at all times. Management, as well as part-time clerks, must adhere to package inspections as they leave the premises.

To combat this human propensity for stealing, employers primarily rely on two methods: lie detector tests, although some states prohibit such testing for pre-employment screening, and paper and pencil "integrity" tests.

Just how far our society has come on business ethics, and stealing in particular, was brought home to me recently in a comment from my son, who was asked to take one of these "integrity" tests before part-time employment at a local supermarket. At dinner he confided to his father and me: "I'm kind of worried about that test they had me take today. They had questions like: 'Have you ever taken drugs?' 'Do you drink alcohol?' 'Have you ever cheated in school?' 'Have you ever stolen money from your parents?' 'Have you ever stolen anything from a schoolmate or an employer?' When I started answering no to all those questions, I started worrying that they'd think I was lying because I sounded too good to be true."

Although his concern was unfounded and he did get the job, I had to reflect on the state of a society where teenagers feel uneasy about being too honest!

We see a breakdown in morality and open acceptance of crooked practices everywhere, whether it's stealing a job by falsifying a resume and buying a diploma for $500 or making personal copies on the company copier. I see children with no models, no standards, no discipline, and no respect for an authority who tells them stealing is wrong.

Although employers are currently coming to grips with the problem by offering training in the form of videos and seminar discussions to inform employees of the seriousness of being caught, many still ponder the question, "Can you train an employee to be honest?"

Perhaps employees can be informed about policies and penalties, but motivation for honesty comes only from inner conviction. Whatever the temptation—long-distance phone calls, a box of pencils, a soiled piece of clothing, padded expense accounts, chocolate éclairs, access to the Dow Jones News Retrieval Service—"You shall not steal" covers them all.

For Further Reflection:

> To be a partner of a thief is to hate one's own life;
> one hears the victim's curse, but discloses nothing.
> (Prov. 29:24 NRSV)

> What you gain by doing evil won't help you at all,
> but being good can save you from death.
> (Prov. 10:2 CEV)

> It's better to be honest and poor
> than to be dishonest and rich. (Prov. 16:8 CEV)

> Being greedy causes trouble for your family
> but you protect yourself by refusing bribes.
> (Prov. 15:27 CEV)

> It's better to be poor and live right,
> than to be rich and dishonest. (Prov. 28:6 CEV)

The Author of Creativity

For in Him we live and move and have our being,
as also some of your own poets have said,
"For we are also His offspring."
(Acts 17:28)

In the beginning when God created the heavens
and the earth, the earth was a formless void
and darkness covered the face of the deep, while a wind
from God swept over the face of the waters. Then God said,
"Let there be light"; and there was light.
(Gen. 1:1–3 NRSV)

"Everything that can be invented has been invented."
That comment was made by Charles Duell, Director of the United States Patent Office — in 1899.

Who would have thought that by the 1990s we'd have mud wrestling, no-fault divorce, plea bargaining for criminals, music by computers, soyburgers, men's perfume, compact discs, garage-door openers, diet pills, surrogate mothers, video telephones, notebook computers, and personal shopper services?

A young clerk had the idea of opening a store that would sell only nickel and dime items. In his own mind, he had figured all the angles. He would run the store, and his boss could supply the money for the inventory and operating capital. No deal, the boss responded upon hearing the idea. Finding that many items to sell for a nickel or dime would be impossible. But F. W. Woolworth certainly made a go on his own.

Most of us, however, are afraid to roll with our ideas. My brother called yesterday, wanting my reaction to a new business start-up idea. After explaining his creative concept and assuring me that there was nothing like it in the Dallas/Fort Worth area, he asked if I'd heard of anyone starting such a business elsewhere. When I assured him I hadn't, the tone in his voice was one of disappointment rather than pleasure. His reasoning? If no one else had thought of this business concept, the idea was probably unsound.

Why do we doubt our own perception and creativity? It's highly likely that none of us, my brother included, has thought enough about what being made in God's own image means.

Certainly, the most striking example of creativity is described in Genesis. From nothing, God created something. Because the Bible tells us that we live and exist by His power, we, too, can participate in divine creativity if we permit God to use us in this way. Certainly the young prophet Daniel came up with a creative way to meet the king of Babylon's requirement that his captives be physically fit. Likewise, when two women both claiming to be the mother of the same child came to King Solomon, he came up with a creative way of determining the real mother.

God is equally ready to help His present-day followers with creative ideas and solutions.

Using our innate creative natures is not a new focus in modern-day business. Way back in 1937, General Electric began a creative engineering program for employees who proved promising within their first two months of employment. And in 1954, the Creative Education Foundation of Buffalo, New York, was founded to teach creativity to corporations. Since that time, creativity training has become almost a fad, and even the largest companies—including Exxon, IBM, General Motors, Colgate-Palmolive, and Shell Oil—have paid consultants as much as $5,000 a day to teach their employees how to think creatively.

Even though experts can't agree on a definition of creativity, they all conclude that we can develop and use our creativity by practicing a few techniques.

Brainstorming. Groups or individuals generate as many ideas as they can to solve a problem. All ideas are recorded—no evaluation or criticism is permitted at this idea stage. Then the participants cluster and categorize the ideas, evaluate their potential, and recommend the best solutions.

Synectics. The two men who set forth this method of creative thinking (George Price and W. J. J. Gordon) are making the strange familiar. Let me oversimplify this method: A problem is analyzed and then reinterpreted in terms of an analogy. A new viewpoint is defined and superimposed over the original problem to frame a new way of looking at the problem and solution. For example, if sunlight interacts with chlorophyll to make plants green, what would it take to react with X substance to make this product turn a different color?

Brainwriting. This technique, developed by Bernd Rohrback, is relatively simple. After a problem or situation is presented, individuals are given a blank piece of paper and asked to write four or five solutions, suggestions, or merely thoughts about the problem or situation. They then exchange the paper with someone else and continue the process by writing additional thoughts they generate from reading the previous person's thoughts.

Lists. Individuals are given a checklist of questions or topic prompts. The items on the checklist act as cues to spur the individuals into new ways of considering a problem. For example: If we are thinking of a new way to print a newsletter, we might come up with new ideas for uses, audience, and content by moving through a checklist that asks these questions: "Can it be made smaller or larger? Can it be a different color? Can it be made with a different piece of equipment? Can it serve more than one purpose? Should it be done quicker? Should it be done slower? Could it be done cheaper? Could it be done more expensively?" These generic questions push people into the creative realm.

Lateral thinking. Lateral thinking encourages people to move out of the mode of logical reasoning. Instead, individuals try to rearrange the information they have about a situation and discard old assumptions about what can and can't be done. Primarily, they challenge all "givens" to a situation and develop new ways of looking at a problem.

For example, the problem or situation might be presented: "We cannot keep large sums of money on the premises. How can we find a dependable van driver to deliver our money to the bank on schedule four times a day?" Participants begin to challenge that line of thinking and those logical assumptions: Why can't we keep large sums of money on the premises? Why drive the money to a bank? Could we use a plane rather than a van? Why four times a day? Maybe we should not deal in cash at all. Maybe we need to move off these premises.

Force-Fitting. This creative-thinking technique encourages individuals to take two seemingly unrelated ideas, even outrageous ideas, and jam them together into one solution — modifying, squeezing, twisting, reducing, or enlarging the ideas to see if they can possibly be made into a reasonable solution or an altogether new option. For example: How could you make stationery smell nice? How could you talk on the phone while driving? We know the results of those force-fitted ideas, but here's another one still under development: How can you eat all the high-calorie foods you desire and still look slim and be healthy?

How do these creative-thinking techniques sound to you? Before you answer that, let me mention how personality and environment fit into the picture.

Creativity seems to flourish in environments where there are both freedom to think and guided control toward a purpose. There have to be sufficient resources, a high level of trust, acceptance of failure, the opportunity to try again for success, and open communication with others. People who flourish in these environments are those who are self-motivated to be the best they can be and to do the best they can do, who have good analytical skills, and who aren't afraid to make mistakes.

Consider the reverse. Creativity is usually stifled in an environment where things are tightly controlled, where no one has the money or the time to think, where people are not rewarded for doing their best. People who are inflexible, who lack motivation, and who have little expertise or experience stifle their own creative impulses.

Therefore, as Christian businesspeople wanting to use the creativity God gave us, we should make sure our offices, churches, and homes foster creative thinking.

Around the office, perhaps we should change statements such as: *"I don't want those file cabinets in here; they look terrible"* to *"How can we keep the necessary data close by yet improve the looks of the office?"* Or: *"How can we get every employee here promptly at 8:00 A.M.?"* to *"How can we set a daily schedule that will ensure that we get our work done satisfactorily?"*

Around our churches, maybe we should change statements such as: *"How can we get everyone here for Wednesday night Bible study?"* to *"How can we get everyone motivated to study the Bible at least two hours during the week?"* Or: *"How can we get enough workers signed up to sponsor this youth retreat?"* to *"What kind of youth retreat would generate maximum participation from, and interaction with, both youth and the adult sponsors?"*

Around our homes, maybe we should change statements such as: *"I don't want Bill to set foot in this house again"* to *"What could we do to encourage Bill to be more considerate when he comes for the weekend?"* Or: *"You're not getting more than $5 a week from your mother and me to spend on junk"* to *"How could you make more of your own spending money?"* Or: *"What kind of work/savings plan per week would you need to be able to buy a stereo with your own money by May 1?"*

With the Author of creativity on our side, we Christians should never lack for creative ways to help our world and to spread the Gospel. Creativity is often simply a matter of seeing through His eyes.

For Further Reflection:

> Therefore, if anyone is in Christ, he is a new creation; old things are passed away; behold, all things have become new. (2 Cor. 5:17)

> In the beginning God created the heavens and the earth. (Gen. 1:1)

> You are worthy, O Lord,
> To receive glory and honor and power;
> For You created all things,
> And by Your will they exist and were created. (Rev. 4:11)

> All things were made through Him, and without Him nothing was made that was made. (John 1:3)

> Create in me a clean heart, O God,
> And renew a steadfast spirit within me. (Ps. 51:10)

The Two-Career Family: Part 1

Who can find a virtuous wife?
For her worth is far above rubies.
The heart of her husband safely trusts her;
So he will have no lack of gain.
She does him good and not evil
All the days of her life.
She seeks wool and flax,
And willingly works with her hands.
She is like the merchant ships,
She brings her food from afar.
She also rises while it is yet night,
And provides food for her household,
And a portion for her maidservants.
She considers a field and buys it;
From her profits she plants a vineyard.
She girds herself with strength,
And strengthens her arms.
She perceives that her merchandise is good,
And her lamp does not go out by night.
She stretches out her hands to the distaff,
And her hand holds the spindle.
She extends her hand to the poor,
Yes, she reaches out her hands to the needy.
She is not afraid of snow for her household,
For all her household is clothed with scarlet.
She makes tapestry for herself;
Her clothing is fine linen and purple.
Her husband is known in the gates,
When he sits among the elders of the land.

She makes linen garments and sells them,
And supplies sashes for the merchants.
Strength and honor are her clothing;
She shall rejoice in time to come.
She opens her mouth with wisdom,
And on her tongue is the law of kindness.
She watches over the ways of her household,
And does not eat the bread of idleness.
Her children rise up and call her blessed;
Her husband also, and he praises her:
"Many daughters have done well,
But you excel them all."
Charm is deceitful and beauty is passing,
But a woman who fears the LORD, she shall be praised.
Give her of the fruit of her hands,
And let her own works praise her in the gates.
(Prov. 31:10–31)

Probably no other issue affecting the family has had so much press coverage in the last twenty years as women joining the work force en masse. In fact, women now comprise 46 percent of the total U.S. civilian work force. Over half (52 percent) of all women are now employed outside the home. And a whopping 78 percent of all women between the ages of 18 and 34 (in other words, mothers) hold a job outside the home.

We've read conflicting reports from clergy, psychologists, schoolteachers, and counselors about the effects of that transition on our society. While some cite studies to show that children in homes where both parents work are brighter, more secure, more responsible, and more cooperative, other spokespersons lay almost all the evils of America at the doorstep of working women.

Whether a woman is the sole means of support for herself and her children due to a disabled, absent, or unwilling-to-work husband, or whether a woman works because she and her family consider it part of God's plan for their lives, the fact remains: The majority of women have taken on an additional role to go with their traditional role.

In Proverbs, we find a virtuous woman who has assumed two roles. She tends well to the ways of her household and husband, and she buys and sells fields and merchandise. Evidently she is successful in both roles to the extent that she is praised for her efforts. This is definitely not the picture of a harried household, unhappy, maladjusted children, and a hostile husband. So how does she do it?

Dara (name changed to protect the guilty) was panicky as she waved me out of her house after I brought over a package left with me by UPS. Her husband was bringing home dinner guests, and the sight wasn't encouraging. She had rattles and stuffed animals from wall to wall, patterns of bunny-rabbit costumes cut from old newspapers slung over the dining room table, piles of unfolded laundry on the sofa, strings all over the carpet, stacks of dishes from the sink to the refrigerator, empty milk cartons and cereal boxes on the breakfast-nook windowsill, and three red negligees hanging over the Japanese partition into the hallway (she sold lingerie on the side).

No, Dara did not consider herself a working woman. She spent her days volunteering for church and school projects, directing her community drama club (the bunny costumes), playing tennis, and campaigning on behalf of a city council representative

Disorganization and priority pile-ups happen to the best. Stay-at-home wives and mothers don't necessarily have clean, organized homes and well-adjusted, happy children and husbands anymore than their counterparts in the business world. And they don't necessarily stay at home all day.

Therefore, women who assume both the traditional and the additional roles should stop flagellating themselves because they can't get it all done and find ways to improve the quality of life for all the family.

I call it hands-on experience with inventory control, project management, delegation and supervision, accountability, and quality control.

Inventory Control

My daughter's favorite trick used to be to leave a note on the dinner table saying, "I need panty hose for school in the morning" or "I'm supposed to have a girl's gift to exchange at gym class at 2:25 today." With a supermarket and drugstore on every corner, children (and sometimes adults) do not realize the inefficiency of running out of things.

Don't be caught up in operating an errand-and-delivery service at your house. Keep adequate stock of the necessities—whether it's cans of tomato juice or shoelaces. (I didn't say buying a birthday gift before you know who the birthday girl is, is easy — just efficient!)

Keep a running list of items that are low and grab it whenever you start out the door to do errands.

Project Management

We do it for vacations; we can do it for the smaller projects. Before we leave on a trip, don't we usually consider what has to be done, when, with what, and by whom?

Apply the same principles to other projects, whether it's to attend a two-day meeting at your church or to shop for school clothes.

My mother is still the best manager of family projects I've ever encountered. On the morning of Christmas Eve, she always orchestrated a clean-up-the-house, pack-the-food, wrap-the-gifts, and dress-for-the-day family marathon that you wouldn't believe any four people could accomplish before noon — the time all of us had to get in the car to go to my grandmother's house for the festivities. And she routinely applied project management ideas weekly to our household.

Although she worked outside the home, she managed to organize us so that we could eat meals together, get the laundry done, and finish homework in time for all of us to attend my brother's and my own basketball, football, baseball, and volleyball games three to four times each week, year-round.

Her secret? Planning.

Delegation and Supervision

Working mothers soon learn the difference between assigning chores and delegation. Assigning children chores is: "Johnny, I want you to carry out the trash this minute. Don't forget the trash can in the hall bathroom. And be sure to tie up the bag with those stronger twist ties."

Delegating is: "Johnny, your responsibility is to put out all the trash each week. The garbage collectors come before noon on Mondays and Thursdays." It's up to Johnny to decide when and how it's done — just as long as the desired results are achieved. And that brings us to the next point.

Accountability

Family members who are responsible for various family projects learn from them. They not only learn to work, they learn to plan, to make decisions, to budget their time, to be successful.

My daughter's accountability training has proven embarrassing to her from time to time. For going on ten years now, she has remembered the following phone conversation:

I phoned her friend Lori, with whom my daughter was spending the night. "Lori, would you please tell Lisa that she needs to come home for the evening."

"Okay, but what happened? Something wrong?"

"Yes, there is. I told her earlier in the day she had to load the dishwasher before she could leave the house again. And I just checked. The kitchen's still not clean. So she'll need to come back home to finish the job."

"You mean she can't spend the night? For that?"

"That's right."

"You're serious?"

"I'm serious. Would you please give her that message?"

Lisa got on the phone. "Mother, Lori and her mother think that's dumb. Nobody has to come home just because of the dishes."

We finished the conversation. She came home to load the dishwasher. She learned. She remembered. She has remembered for a long, long time. In fact, she laughingly reminded me of this incident the last time she came home from college, in the midst of a conversation about how tidy her apartment always seems to be.

Through supervision, rewards, and penalties, children learn what it feels like to do a complete project well, to be trusted, to be self-sufficient, to accept direction, to be dependable, to contribute to the common good of the family. In short, they learn to be successful adults.

Quality Control

Mothers most likely are the ones to check up on family atmosphere and goals with, "Hey, are we having fun yet?" In an atmosphere where husband and wife are supposed to be mutually submissive and loving to each other and where children are submissive to their parents, there should be quality life as God defined it for the home. If that is not the case, do some serious questioning.

- Who feels left out?
- Who needs more time from whom?
- Are we watching too much TV?
- What chores can we leave undone with nobody caring?
- Who is involved in too many outside activities at the expense of the family?
- When is the last time we spent a long weekend together?
- When is the last time we as a family participated in an extended worship experience such as a retreat?
- When is the last time we played a game or took in a family movie?
- Is one member of the family doing most of the sacrificing and work to keep things running smoothly?
- Is one member of the family forcing everyone else to sacrifice to keep his or her own schedule and goals on target?
- What are the family's financial goals, educational goals, and spiritual goals for the next five years? What do we *all* have to do to reach them?

Keeping the quality of home life high is no easier than it is in the workplace, but the rewards are worth far more.

Rarely do working wives and mothers have to chastise themselves about "eating the bread of idleness." Instead, we all need to focus on organizing, planning, sharing, and giving attention to quality life. These will mean the difference between a harried home and a haven.

For Further Reflection:

> Whatever your hand finds to do, do it with your might; for there is no work or device or knowledge or wisdom in the grave where you are going. (Eccl. 9:10)

The Two-Career Family: Part 2

Submitting to one another in the fear of God.
Wives, submit to your own husbands, as to the Lord.
For the husband is head of the wife, as also Christ is
head of the church; and He is the Savior of the body.
Therefore, just as the church is subject to Christ, so let
the wives be to their own husbands in everything.
Husbands, love your wives, just as Christ also loved
the church and gave Himself for her.... So husbands
ought to love their own wives as their own bodies;
he who loves his wife loves himself.
(Eph. 5:21–25, 28)

Having just concluded a seminar at 5:00 P.M., I dashed toward the phones in the lobby to call home before heading out into the traffic. At the two busy phones ahead of me were two male executives in standard pinstriped suits and ties. They were involved, I was sure, in some last-minute corporate deal making. As I stood waiting my turn, I couldn't help but overhear both conversations.

The monologue to my left went something like this: "I'm still tied up in a meeting, and I'm not going to be home for dinner. Would you please get my suit out of the cleaners before they close? ... Yeah, I'll meet you there. And one more thing, bring the checkbook."

I glanced to my right to see if the conversation there was winding down. Not much chance. The guy was bent over, scribbling something on a scrap of paper. A new offer in the negotiations? Then I heard, "Yeah, okay, I got it. Two boxes of orange Jell-O . . ."

Needless to say, I smiled approvingly. More and more men are rethinking their roles as husband and father and doing more than just bringing home the bacon. Their jobs today may involve Jell-O, birthday presents, and prescription medicine.

The idea of mutual submission, love, and support between husbands and wives is not new. I saw my grandfather, a salt miner, cattleman, and vegetable farmer, wash the family dishes more than I saw my grandmother do it. He also helped can vegetables, hang out the laundry, and buy the groceries. She, in turn, worked in a factory for years and then, as retirement age approached, took an "easier" job as department store salesclerk. In other words, before they died in their eighties, those two long-time believers learned what love, mutual submission, and mutual support were.

Although pollsters now tell us that most husbands give lip service to the idea that men should participate in household responsibilities, for some, the intention or belief has not become reality. What do I mean by *participate?* How can husbands really tune in to their families' needs?

Emotional Support

Some men still think their own on-the-job pressures and schedule hassles should have top priority. When a child complains about having difficulty with his math teacher, instead of listening and understanding, the father's response is: "Well, son, you're just going to have to deal with that. Out in the real world like I face every day ..."

When a wife attempts to share a work problem, rather than listening or offering practical advice, her husband cuts his eyes back to the newspaper with: "Well, just quit then. You don't have to work." That kind of comment tells the wife that her problems are minimal and petty compared to his, that she is bringing it all upon herself by taking on what she can't handle.

Emotional support means taking the feelings of all family members as seriously as your own.

Verbal Encouragement

A selfish husband usually belittles a wife's bonus as "better than nothing," downplays the promotion as "the least they could do," and insists the two-day training sessions away from home are an interruption and imposition on his personal schedule. A participating husband shares his wife's excitement over a promotion, a chance at more education, a raise or bonus, an opportunity to travel and broaden her experiences, or a position on a worthwhile committee.

In fact, my husband celebrates even my "little" career successes and opportunities. After I presented my first public workshop on a new subject, he surprised me with the gift of a watch. The note attached read: "It's TIME the world realized what you have to offer." This for no occasion other than a tiny milestone.

That's encouragement — unsolicited and genuine.

Sharing Excitement and Defeats

A participating husband lets his wife know when he's about to close a big deal or when he blows the presentation and doesn't pull it off as planned. He calls home while he's attending a convention in Miami to tell her about the best restaurant meal he's ever eaten, and brings her a small gift to say she was missed. He sums up the day's meetings, knowing she is an intelligent person who appreciates his expertise.

A selfish husband brushes off questions from a concerned wife with, "You wouldn't understand" or "I don't have time to go into it with you."

When I occasionally ask an acquaintance or friend what her husband does for a living, I'm always amazed how many times I get answers such as, "He works for XYZ Company; I don't know exactly what he does there. Something to do with oil." I didn't say I was amazed at the *wife's* lack of concern or ignorance; poor communication can often be traced to a husband who doesn't care enough about participating in the family to include his wife in his day-to-day life. Wives have been warned to expect this kind of silent treatment if their husbands work for the CIA or the underworld, but not if their husbands have normal jobs.

Help with the Mental and Menial Tasks

Although I appreciated the supportive executive husband who was stopping by the store for two boxes of Jell-O, somebody had to remember the promise to take the Jell-O salad to the church dinner and call him with a reminder. Sometimes, for the working mother, the problem is not so much the effort of actually wrapping the birthday present; it's the responsibility of deciding how much you can afford to spend, finding out what the child wants or needs, and telephone shopping for the best price. Going by the store to pick up the gift may be the least of the effort.

A nonparticipating husband does only what he's asked. He vacuums up the mulch spilled on the carpet and takes out the garbage. A participating husband, on the other hand, assumes overall responsibility for some things—the remembering as well as the actual doing. He helps to see that the house is clean before the in-laws arrive, remembers to take your daughter to get her proper immunizations before school starts, or sends a "care package" of cookies to your son away at college.

Who takes care of vacation plans and surprise weekends away? If it's always the same person, ask yourself why.

Quality Control

Finally, a participating husband checks the results of his emotional support, his praise and encouragement, their sharing of mutual concerns and responsibilities. Are all family members happy? Are all communicating? Are all spending quality time together as a family? Is the family meeting financial, emotional, and spiritual goals? If not, why not?

It may be up to the participating, mutually submissive husband to let the family, especially his wife, know when they're not getting a good return on their investment. "Hey, hon, why are you spending so much time in the kitchen on the weekends? Why don't we have sandwiches or Chinese take-out more often? I'd rather have you sitting in here with the kids and me."

Check out even the "together" activities occasionally. When the kids are home from college, we usually plan a full weekend — from waterskiing to movies to eating out to shopping the flea markets to jogging in 10K runs. But occasionally, we get so worn out we all opt for sleeping in and lounging around the patio, with nothing more demanding involved than walking to the mailbox.

The idea is to monitor everybody's needs, likes, and dislikes. We all need space and we all need togetherness. Sorting out which comes when is the responsibility of everyone, particularly the husband/father.

To love a wife and family as Christ loved the church often requires more investment than bringing home two boxes of orange Jell-O. But the emotional and spiritual return outperforms all other investments.

For Further Reflection:

> But if anyone does not provide for his own, and especially for those of his household, he has denied the faith and is worse than an unbeliever. (1 Tim. 5:8)

Lying and Living with the Boss

Lying lips are an abomination to the LORD,
But those who deal truthfully are His delight.
(Prov. 12:22)

Getting treasures by a lying tongue
Is the fleeting fantasy of those who seek death.
(Prov. 21:6)

The majority of us don't butt our heads against big lies involving nonexistent corporate takeover plans or trade secrets. Rather, we deal with "small-scale" lies that make everyone wary.

An Excuse Booth provides patrons of bars across the United States with just what they'll need to get back into the office without questions. This Excuse Booth is a TV sound studio in a phone booth. For a nominal fee it will play background noises of your choosing while you offer your lie to the person on the other end of the line.

If you want to use flight cancellations and delays as an excuse, you can select airport announcements and jet takeoff and landing noises. If you want to blame the weather, you can select the rainstorm effect. If you're supposedly attending a retirement gala, the background tape creates an instant party, complete with laughter, conversation, and clinking glasses.

But, you may be thinking, lying is a way of life only for office deadbeats, for husbands and wives cheating on their spouses, or for drunks and drug addicts holing up in these bars with their Excuse Booths.

Lying, however, has become a way of life for many pinstriped Christians as well.

You have a problem: You're late for the meeting — again. The truth is that you and a friend got to talking golf over Chinese food and simply didn't get back to the office on time. The solution: Have your secretary tell your client that you were called out suddenly for an emergency. The result: Your client will rarely believe it, but she will nod and smile knowingly, remembering the last time she used the same line.

You have a phone call from someone you'd rather not talk to. The solution is delivered through your secretary: "He's in conference right now." "She's in a meeting." "He's on the other line." The result: Loss of productivity for both your office and the caller because both will have to call and respond several more times before the message is clear. The truth is easier. Conveyed through you or your secretary, it might be: "I'm not interested in the product (service) at this time," or "I'm very involved on a project this afternoon. May I call you back tomorrow?" Or "I don't have the information you need, but I suggest you call Ellen Brown."

Business owners lie to their suppliers and customers about delivery dates, prices, discounts, and terms. I'll have to admit that I suffer from a bad case of naivete and still tend to take people at their word—especially those who represent large reputable companies. Recently, we met with a prospective client from a top Fortune 50 company, who had asked us to submit a proposal for some design work and the follow-up training for a major project. In the meeting, the buyer stated that he hadn't expected to see any charges for the design work. We should "absorb" whatever time we spent to do the design work, he said, because the pending contract was so large. When I explained that we would have to spend several days in the design phase and that we intended to charge for such work, he stated that none of the other bidders had included such charges in their proposal.

I took him at his word.

As we left the meeting, a colleague of the buyer's who'd also been in the meeting stepped into the elevator with us. "I feel compelled to tell you that he's lying. All the other bidders have included such charges in their bid."

To say it happens every day still does not lessen the impact of hearing a responsible person in a high position in a major corporation boldly lie.

Publishers habitually lie in their advertisements to store owners about how many copies of a book they print.

Accountants lie to their company creditors with the cliché we all love to hate, "Your check is in the mail."

Salespeople, falling short of slanderous comments, misrepresent and lie about their competitors' products and services. When one tells the truth, the impact makes you want to buy on the spot.

We recently moved into new offices, and the salesperson from the office furniture company botched the order from beginning to end. The first shipment of workstations arrived later than promised. When the shipment arrived, the countertops were the wrong width. The second shipment came in the wrong color. Some required pieces were missing altogether. All made for the perfect opportunity to lie: "The manufacturer sent the wrong stuff." But to our surprise, upon opening the shipment, the salesperson left to call his office and then returned with this confession: "I rechecked the paperwork; it wasn't the manufacturer. It was my error. I myself misordered the items."

The truth is so seldom used that he won our respect, despite the mistakes. We'll do business with him again.

Buyers lie to sellers. Not long ago we conducted a public seminar for which a lawyer registered to attend by charging the fee to his credit card. The brochure stated that full refunds would be given until a certain date; no refunds would be given for cancellations later than that date. At 8:00 P.M. the evening before the seminar, the lawyer called to cancel his registration. I happened to be working late and took the call myself—although I didn't identify myself. The lawyer stated that he had a case coming to trial the Tuesday following the seminar, earlier than he had expected, and he would need the weekend to prepare. I repeated the no-refund policy, but offered to mail the seminar materials to him. He said that would be fine.

A week later, we received a call from the lawyer, followed by a copy of the letter he sent to his credit card company instructing it to reverse the registration charges. He went on to explain that the "clerk" who took his call that evening had promised him a full refund because he had "a trial _in progress_ and therefore could not attend the next day's seminar."

Business owners face such shenanigans daily.

Bookkeepers lie to auditors with their alterations and their explanations about their reasoning. SEC regulations require every public company "to make and keep books, records, and accounts, which, in reasonable detail, accurately and fairly reflect the transactions and dispositions of the assets of the issue." Playing games with a petty-cash voucher or an employee time card is an illegal lie. And what's more, computers that disguise altered records make the temptation to lie even stronger.

Allen I. Young, now deputy general counsel at Price Waterhouse, pointed out in _Price Waterhouse Review_ the fraud and danger in what is termed "cute accounting" or "loopholing." If caught, the people who lie in these ways can always point out a chapter and verse in accounting literature that, they claim, led them to such erroneous thinking. Their rationalizations rarely wash with the IRS because the IRS knows they are following only the letter of the law rather than the substance.

People misuse their business positions of authority for personal gain. An acquaintance completed the research for his entire dissertation by misrepresenting his purpose. When he called to interview consultants, he used his company name and led secretaries to believe he was calling about a work project. Only when he got the interviewees on the phone did he admit that his reason for calling was the dissertation.

It's not that most of us aren't aware of God's attitude about all corporate lying but that, unlike the psalmist, we haven't made this verse our prayer: "Remove from me the way of lying, / And grant me Your law graciously" (Ps. 119:29).

To term all such situations as lying sounds a little harsh because we generally sort falsehoods into several categories: whoppers, black lies, white lies, and half-truths. I'm not sure God does.

For Further Reflection:

> A false witness will not go unpunished,
> And he who speaks lies will not escape. (Prov. 19:5)

> What is desirable in a person is loyalty, and it is better to be poor than a liar. (Prov. 19:22 NRSV)

> Do not be a witness against your neighbor without cause,
> For would you deceive with your lips? (Prov. 24:28)

> We trap ourselves by telling lies,
> but we stay out of trouble by living right.
> We are rewarded or punished for what we say and do.
> (Prov. 12:13–14 CEV)

> Good people have kind thoughts, but you should never trust the advice of someone evil. (Prov. 12:5 CEV)

An honest person tells the truth in court, but a dishonest person tells nothing but lies. (Prov. 12:17 CEV)

Truth will last forever; lies are soon found out. (Prov. 12:19 CEV)

Therefore, putting away lying, "Let each one of you speak truth with his neighbor," for we are members of one another. (Eph. 4:25)

Delegation and Letting Della Do It

The next day Moses sat as usual to hear the people's
complaints against each other, from morning to evening.
When Moses' father-in-law saw how much time this was
taking, he said, "Why are you trying to do all this alone,
with people standing here all day long to get your help? . . .
Moses, this job is too heavy a burden for you to try to
handle all by yourself. Now listen, and let me give you
a word of advice, and God will bless you. . . .
"Find some capable, godly, honest men who hate bribes,
and appoint them as judges. . . . Let these men
be responsible to serve the people with justice at all times.
Anything that is too important or complicated can be
brought to you. But the smaller matters they can take care
of themselves. That way it will be easier for you because
you will share the burden with them. If you follow
this advice, and if the Lord agrees, you will be able to
endure the pressures, and there will be peace
and harmony in the camp."

(Ex. 18:13–14, 18–19, 21, 22–23 TLB)

Are you irreplaceable?

Do you skip vacations or take your time off only a
couple of days at a time?

Do you try to keep up with everybody's activities and whereabouts rather than simply keeping up with their accomplishments?

Are you working longer hours than you'd like to?

Are people having to transfer around you to move up in the company?

Do you always seem to have somebody waiting to talk to you about something before they can go further with their work?

Do you constantly hear, "I guess we'd better run that by George before we make a final decision"?

Do you manage to phone into the office every day while you're off during an illness or while attending a training class or convention?

Do you have a lot of crises when you're out of the office?

If you answered "yes" to most of these questions, not only are you not practicing the biblical example of management, you may find that you're not pleasing your corporate manager either.

According to Everett T. Suters, author of *Succeed in Spite of Yourself*, senior management does not look favorably on the manager who has become irreplaceable. Irreplaceable managers have become logjams holding up decisions, activities, and the growth of other employees.

That thought often runs contrary to some managers' thinking because many have the wrong concept of delegation. They look on delegation as dumping the undesirable tasks on their employees or as shirking their own responsibilities when they don't have time to get them done. Neither is the case.

Delegation, just as in Moses' day, is a means for developing others to their fullest potential in a way that will help everyone reach the desired goal. Women employees seem to have more trouble than men in embracing the value of delegation. Perhaps that's because for so long women have been trained to pick up the slack at home for their husbands and children. A child says, "I got a spot on my shirt that I can't get out." Mother responds, "Just leave it in the sink. I'll see what I can do," rather than referring the child to spot removers or other methods she herself will later try.

She is accepting upward delegation from her children; they tell her what she has to get done.

On the job, senior executives do not want to be delegated to in this manner. They prefer that their managers train their subordinates and coworkers to assume the necessary task themselves.

So what is good delegation as Moses and Jesus practiced it? Delegating is not simply assigning tasks. An assignment is something like: "Print out copies of the last four years' quarterly reports." Delegating is much broader, leading to the accomplishment of a goal. Researchers have outlined several levels of delegation:

- Look into the situation and bring me the facts and alternatives. I'll make the decisions.
- Recommend a decision for my approval.

- Let me know what decision you are making. Do it unless I say not to.
- Take action. Let me know what you did and how it turns out.
- Take action. Let me know only if things didn't work out.
- Take action. You don't need to let me know anything else.

Different parts of the job require different delegation levels. Those managers who stop at the first level are merely assigning tasks; they soon become problems to their organization and everyone concerned.

Here are some *do's* and *don'ts* that will improve your delegation habits.

Do pick the right people for the right jobs. Don't give all the ho-hum jobs to one person and those that give a sense of satisfaction and challenge to the most willing. Assign your people jobs they have been trained to handle.

Do transfer the freedom and the authority that go with the task. Instead of outlining all the steps to be taken, simply explain the results you want, the date they're needed, and the acceptable cost. "Please see that all employees who will attend next week's meeting have copies of report A and report B before Wednesday. Keep the printing and shipping costs below $300." The employee develops his or her own decision-making skills by determining when, where, and how.

Do be specific about the desired results, including time and financial limits. You cannot measure success if you don't make your employees aware of exactly what you want to achieve with the project. Clarify everything. If there are extenuating circumstances and problems, let your employees know from the beginning.

Now for the *don'ts:*

Don't demand perfection. We had an administrative assistant who failed to deposit payroll taxes within the allotted time period at the bank; that mistake cost us severe tax penalties. We've had people buy services we don't need and equipment features we won't use; those misjudgments cost us money. We have all made mistakes.

You have made mistakes; they will make mistakes. But occasional mistakes are no reason to throw the whole process of delegation out the window.

Don't accept upward delegation. In effect, employees delegate to their bosses with phrases such as, "I don't know if we should buy Brand X or Brand Y computers for this office. What do you think?" The boss then takes the monkey on his back and assumes responsibility for that decision when he could have responded with, "Why don't you investigate both models and come back to me with your recommendation."

Jesus spent three years preparing His disciples to carry on the ministry that has been growing for the last 2,000 years in His earthly absence. Have you spent comparable time in developing your own employees who look to you for leadership?

Irreplaceable is not a compliment. It's a trap.

For Further Reflection:

> And the twelve called together the whole community of the disciples and said, "It is not right that we should neglect the word of God in order to wait on tables. Therefore, friends, select from among yourselves seven men of good standing, full of the Spirit and of wisdom, whom we may appoint to this task." (Acts 6:2–3 NRSV)

Feeling Fine and the
Daniel Dilemma

I keep my body under control and make it my slave,
so I won't lose out after telling the good news to others.
(1 Cor. 9:27 CEV)

It is vain for you to rise up early,
To sit up late,
To eat the bread of sorrows;
For so He gives His beloved sleep.
(Ps. 127:2)

You look at your watch, and it's 7:00 P.M. The sentences you're composing for the proposal sound like so much gibberish on the yellow legal pad. How can you possibly get it finished, get on the plane tomorrow afternoon to fly to San Francisco, and present it to your biggest prospective customer? Besides that, you're hungry, you're exhausted, and you're guilty — of promising your son you'd catch a few throws and then not being home before dark. You begin to feel inefficient. How do other people do it?

They've learned that stamina starts with your attitude. Stamina comes in a controlled way when you learn to break fatiguing habits and learn new ones — ones that keep you fit for both the physical and emotional endurance tests you face on the job.

But, you may ask, doesn't fatigue go with the territory? And don't many people do their best work under pressure? No, to both questions.

Fatigue comes from both psychological and physical sources. As busy employees, we work long hours under emotional pressure. But mental work involves little physical exhaustion; it's the emotional stress of travel, conflicts, decisions, and deadlines that saps our energy.

Fatigue leads to inefficiency, distorted perceptions, lowered standards, poor decisions, loss of initiative, and emotional lows. According to Mortimer R. Feinberg and Aaron Levenstein in their *Wall Street Journal* article "Building Endurance," psychologists noted during World War II that pilots made the most errors as they returned to land after a dangerous raid. The analysts pinpointed the cause as the pilots' tendency at the point of fatigue to relax their standards of performance quality and accuracy. Fatigue does the same to businesspeople, making them unable to judge their slipping performance.

So if fatigue doesn't automatically come with the territory from nine to five, what are its causes? Anger. Failure. Boredom. Poor eating habits. Inadequate exercise. Insufficient sleep. The good news is that all of these can be controlled.

Refuse to carry around emotional baggage such as hostility. Learn to slough off the idea of working with someone you find difficult. If you can't limit your contact with that person, at least psych yourself up with the thought, "I'm getting paid $40 an hour to work with that person. A little discomfort is worth it."

If you have failed to meet your own expectations, find the source of that failure and reeducate yourself. Find new resources, new methods, or new goals.

If boredom on the job is the cause, look outside your job for the extra dimension that will recreate excitement and energize your life. Why not work on your spiritual goals if your work gives your mind time to wander? Whom can you minister to? Who needs a helping hand or a listening ear? What can you study, memorize, or reflect on?

The physical causes of fatigue are even easier to correct and control than the emotional causes.

Peter M. Miller, in his book *The Hilton Head Executive Stamina Program*, points out that prolonged mental concentration causes a reduction in muscle glycogen, the blood sugar that serves as stored energy. Our brain is dependent on glucose for mental alertness and stamina. Glucose comes from complex carbohydrates such as fruits, vegetables, breads, cereals, potatoes, and pasta. Our overall diet should contain about 60 percent complex carbohydrates; we need only 15 percent protein.

Now we understand why Daniel (Daniel 1) and his friends were more mentally alert on their simple diet than on the king's rich meats. And notice that Daniel drank only water. The loss of body fluid inside a stuffy, dry office results in lethargy. Fluid loss is even greater when you drink coffee, tea, caffeinated colas, or alcohol.

Power lunches aren't what they used to be. In case you haven't noticed, more and more people are making their mid-day meals light. The power comes in their mental alertness. In fact, I'm continually amazed at how many people eat only fruit or fruit and vegetables for lunch solely for the purpose of alertness during the afternoon.

In addition to eating and drinking correctly, we need exercise — at least 20 to 30 minutes every day. You don't have time to exercise? You don't have time *not* to exercise. Exercise keeps you mentally alert so you can accomplish more in less time. From a rather sedentary life in my thirties, I began to ride a bicycle, then walk, then jog. Last year, my husband and I ran the 12K Bay to Breakers race in San Francisco, and then I won a first-place trophy in our own local 10K run. (Of course, there were only two runners in my age category!) The point is, you can start from flab and move to fit at almost any age.

Many CEOs believe that staying healthy and physically fit is vital to their continued success and that of all their employees. Consequently, they maintain a daily exercise routine and often establish health and fitness centers at their company facilities. They claim that a fitness program helps them build stamina to meet the physical demands of running a company. Exercise programs for all employees help foster team spirit and cooperation and promote a balanced business and personal life.

Some companies even encourage employees to use the corporate fitness facilities by giving them an extra thirty minutes at lunch period to exercise. They are allowed to wear casual clothes in the afternoon after their workout. Other companies provide financial incentives for employees who exercise, lose weight, or quit smoking. Staying in top physical condition is top priority.

If even the corporate world realizes the value of physical fitness, shouldn't Christians be leading the pack?

The writer of Ecclesiastes noted that the race is not always to the swift. The real test is to keep running.

For Further Reflection:

> I beseech you therefore, brethren, by the mercies of God, that you present your bodies a living sacrifice, holy, acceptable to God, which is your reasonable service. (Rom. 12:1)

> Beloved, I pray that you may prosper in all things and be in health, just as your soul prospers. (3 John 2)

Are Leaders Born or Does God Create Them on the Job?

For the leaders of this people cause them to err,
And those who are led by them are destroyed.
(Isa. 9:16)

Where are the future leaders of corporate America, a correspondent to Ann Landers wanted to know. Is it the "yellow peril" we should fear? Warren Bennis, widely acclaimed management consultant, professor in the School of Business Administration at the University of Southern California, and author of *On Becoming a Leader,* responded to the inquirer:

Japan, which is about the size of Montana, supports 115 million people. The largest automobile manufacturer in the world is not General Motors, it is Toyota.

Eight of the ten largest banks in the world (in terms of assets) are in Japan. (Citicorp, the only American bank on the list, is third.)

In Japan, students attend school 240 days a year as compared with 180 days in the United States. . . . Ninety-seven percent of Japan's students finish high school. In Chicago, it's about 50 percent, and about half of those who do finish cannot read at a high school level. The illiteracy rate in Japan is less than 1 percent. Ours is about 27 percent.

The Japanese value their young people and their elderly. Strong emphasis is placed on education and family. Respect for teachers and parents is deeply embedded in their culture.

Bennis concludes that we have little to fear from the Japanese model but much to learn. The harsh words now being exchanged between Japanese and American workers focus on blame rather than improvement. Our future, however, rests on improvement. To whom can we turn to lead the way?

If the Bible teaches anything about leadership, it teaches that leaders are made. Businesspeople can learn to lead those around them to meet corporate goals as well as God's goals for their lives.

At the beginning of his career, Moses had no experience, a sinful past (he'd murdered an Egyptian), no authority over or respect from the people ("the people won't listen to me, Lord"), and at least one serious weakness in his job skills (his stammering speech). All he had were connections. God had provided for his upbringing in the palace by Pharaoh's daughter, but those connections didn't bring Moses success in leading God's people to the Promised Land. Moses *learned* to lead.

The disciples are yet another example of what God does with men who are willing to become leaders. With little money and less political acumen, they turned the first-century world upside down.

So what does it take to be a real leader who serves God and the corporation?

Leaders are idea people. They don't necessarily run with the crowd; they turn the crowd. They focus on what to do and when to do it, not whom to blame for trouble or inaction.

Leaders take risks. They look at the possible rewards and confidently take action. They do not tie their egos to possible failure, allowing others to learn from their mistakes.

Leaders develop their followers. Army Chief of Staff General C. Marshall advised his colleagues to make their subordinates self-reliant: "If you want a man to be for you, never let him feel he is dependent on you. Make him feel you are in some way dependent on him." Leaders learn their employees' strengths and appreciate them for those abilities. They find ways to praise and reward them and push them to develop their potential in weak areas. They are clear in their directions, firm with their goals and procedures.

In leading people to attain their highest potential, leaders keep their people informed, give them purpose, and generate excitement about the tasks to be completed. They shine the spotlight on their staff performers and let them know what it feels like to be on the front edge of success — in the small things as well as the big things. Leaders generate energy for and urgency about a job well done.

Leaders take the time to get to know their people personally. They are available to them. They listen to their questions. They are sensitive to their disappointments and fears. They let them be humans, not machines.

Does such sensitivity make a difference in followers' attitudes? You bet. An accountant for a large oil company recently told me, "I've resigned my job and will be leaving next week. Frankly, I'm very good at what I do. My boss knows it, and he sends everybody else in the department to me for help with their work. But I never get any recognition for what I do. All the reports I prepare are for his signature, and I'm tired of making him look literate. I'm tired of carrying his lunch."

Leaders are always around to give support. Leaders are not hit-and-run delegators. They do not dump an assignment and leave a subordinate to sink or swim without providing appropriate psychological support for the completion of the task. They empower an employee to act — through information, through example, through training, through monetary resources, through accountability for results.

In one of our workshops, we discuss critical questions to be asked or answered in delegating a writing project. I pose the question to attendees: "When bosses don't provide the answers to these critical questions, why don't you just ask?" The common answer is, "I don't want to look stupid."

Leaders verify that their instructions are understood and give their followers freedom to ask questions. In other words, the development of a subordinate does not mean finding someone to blame in case things go wrong; it means finding someone to praise when things go right. Leaders empower others and then praise them for results.

In short, leaders need to foster competence, integrity, and optimism about the work to be done.

Learn to be that leader U.S. corporations need so desperately. Look for opportunities to turn into ideas, be willing to take risks for rewards, and develop subordinates to their fullest potential, making them feel significant and offering your support. When you consider Moses' forty years of apprenticeship in the wilderness, it's not too late to start your own leadership-learning curve.

For Further Reflection:

In time of civil war there are many leaders, but a sensible leader restores law and order. (Prov. 28:2 CEV)

When justice rules a nation, everyone is glad; when injustice rules, everyone groans. . . .
An honest ruler makes the nation strong; a ruler who takes bribes will bring it to ruin. (Prov. 29:2, 4 CEV)

But Moses said to God, "Who am I that I should go to Pharaoh, and that I should bring the children of Israel out of Egypt?" So He said, "I will certainly be with you. And this shall be a sign to you, that I have sent you: When you have brought the people out of Egypt, you shall serve God on this mountain. (Ex. 3:11–12)

Contented Cows and Curdled Milk

> Not that I speak in regard to need, for I have learned in whatever state I am, to be content: I know how to be abased, and I know how to abound. Everywhere and in all things I have learned both to be full and to be hungry, both to abound and to suffer need. I can do all things through Christ who strengthens me.
>
> (Phil. 4:11–13)

> Now godliness with contentment is great gain.
> (1 Tim. 6:6)

> So do not worry about tomorrow, for tomorrow will bring worries of its own. Today's trouble is enough for today.
> (Matt. 6:34 NRSV)

Is contentment anathema to business? According to many employees and employers, it is. Several years ago, *INC* ran a feature story by the sole proprietor of a small landscape service. Friends were constantly after him to expand his business. But to do so, the owner would have had to go heavily into debt to finance new equipment to handle larger commercial accounts and to hire more staff. He expressed deep satisfaction with handling only residential accounts, because he got to know his customers and was able to take time to get involved, in small ways, in their lives. He concluded that he was making enough money to provide well for his family and that was his goal. As a result, he had few pressures on the job and a lot of time with his family and friends.

His attitude and management style seem to be an anomaly to the entrepreneur. But according to the letters written to the editor after this feature article appeared, this man's contentment and sense of satisfaction proved highly refreshing to the readers. There was and is much to be said for contentment with the status quo.

Contrary to popular belief, "doing without" is not the major cause of discontent; often the problem is doing with more. The more we have, the more we want. We have been swept into the world's bent on "getting." When our *needs* are met, we start on our want list.

A friend of mine, Bob Handly, laughs (now) about his state of mind when he owned a successful executive search firm in Dallas and felt a compulsion to work harder and harder and make more and more. One morning, sitting at his desk stewing over a big decision, he broke out into a cold sweat. He grew clammy. Was this the big heart attack everyone had predicted for his Type-A personality? He paced. He didn't like his life anymore. The fun was gone. Suddenly panicked, he did something he'd never done before. He got in his car and drove home in the middle of the morning. His world grew smaller and smaller, and within six months he was completely housebound. An analyst later helped Bob discover that he was suffering from agoraphobia. Bob's fear of having panic attacks in public places was the result, the analyst said, of Bob's stressful, pressure-cooker life-style. After a long struggle, Bob overcame the phobia, wrote a best-selling book telling his story, and then re-sumed a more reasonable lifestyle and career. Bob's path took him through much pain on the way to contentment.

Is that drive for more and more all bad? Weren't we taught to better ourselves and that each generation of parents should want better things for its children? Yes. But we've learned the lesson too well. We've scaled the wall of improvement and jumped into the lake of discontent. We're drowning in the depths of indebtedness. Instead of following the biblical admonition to owe no man, we owe every man.

Why? We have lost our sense of values, confusing the price of a good pair of jeans with an autographed label. We've confused the comfort and size of a home with an address on the right street. You may recall how much to-do was made about David Souter's "modest" home after his nomination to the Supreme Court. The media showed amazement that someone so successful found himself content with such a "modest lifestyle."

The pursuit of contentment drives us. We've mis-placed our priorities, often putting work before worship and family. We're suffering from misguided giving, confusing our tip to the taxi driver with our tithe for God.

English clergyman Charles Caleb Colton noted that "True contentment depends not on what we have; a tub was large enough for Diogenes, but a world was too little for Alexander."

Discontent is like paint splattered over a once-clean windowpane. It mars the view so that the whole place looks vacant, as though it were under construction.

Older employees long for the energy and good health of young new stars on the corporate fast track; young employees long for the experience and contacts of the older. The powerful administrator longs for the peace of mind of the staff member; the staff member longs for the boss's clout. The wealthy long for safety from thieves and charlatan investment advisors; the poor wish for the financial security of the rich.

True contentment is an attitude — an active, creative attitude. Someone has observed that the contented man is never poor while the discontented is never rich. Perhaps we should view our bank balance, work, people, and conditions around us with a new pair of eyes. Contentment leads us to work with a situation until we get everything from it that God has for us.

If you can't get overtime hours and wages, can you use your spare time to develop a stronger relationship with your family or friends? If you can't transfer to a new job and learn a new skill, can you learn new and better ways to do the old job? If your job provides no challenge, and therefore no pressure, can you put your energies into a volunteer project in the church or community?

Although we should never be satisfied with what we *are,* we should always be satisfied with what we *have.* And if you can't honestly say that you've arrived at contentment, don't give up on developing that attitude. The Apostle Paul assured us that he had *learned* contentment. Praise God for what you have and trust Him for what you need.

For Further Reflection:

Two things I request of You (Deprive me not before I die):
Remove falsehood and lies far from me;
Give me neither poverty nor riches—
Feed me with the food allotted to me;
Lest I be full and deny You,
And say, "Who is the LORD?"
Or lest I be poor and steal,
And profane the name of my God. (Prov. 30:7–9)

Let your conduct be without covetousness; be content
with such things as you have. For He Himself has said,
"I will never leave you, nor forsake you." (Heb. 13:5)

Likewise the soldiers asked him, saying, "And what shall
we do?" So he said to them, "Do not intimidate anyone
or accuse falsely, and be content with your wages. (Luke
3:14)

The LORD does not let the righteous go hungry, but he
thwarts the craving of the wicked. (Prov. 10:3 NRSV)

And my God shall supply all your need according to His
riches in glory by Christ Jesus. (Phil. 4:19)

Rejoice in the Lord always. Again I say, rejoice! (Phil. 4:4)

When a man is gloomy, everything seems to go wrong;
when he is cheerful, everything seems right! (Prov.
15:15 TLB)

And the peace of God, which surpasses all understanding, will guard your hearts and minds through Christ
Jesus. (Phil. 4:7)

Right and Stupid

When a good person gives in to the wicked, it's like
dumping garbage in a stream of clear water.
(Prov. 25:26 CEV)

The executive vice-president of a large software
company asked me about obtaining a free preview
of a computer-based sales training program distributed
by my company. Needless to say, I was a little shocked
at the up-front request, because his own company has a
competitive software package on the market.

But he explained this way: "Oh, yeah, I'm still vice
president at XYZ Company. But headquarters is out of
state, and they don't even know what I'm doing down
here. Actually, a few months ago, I began my own
consulting business. And I've got a client overseas that
wants to buy sales training. If your sales package is better
than ours, I've got no qualms about recommending your
program to my client. I'm leaving Company XYZ in the
next few months anyway."

I sent him the free preview package. Several weeks
later, on his new consulting business letterhead, he returned the sales package, saying he decided to recommend another one to his client. At my last contact with
him two years after that, he was *still* vice president of

XYZ Company. And he was still operating a consulting business on somebody else's payroll!

Do businesspeople not hear daily about such unethical things? Certainly, and even much worse. Lying, cheating, murder, drugs, tax scams, abuse, and evil abound these days. We still talk about such things, but what has changed is our way of thinking about such things.

"Greed is all right, by the way. I want you to know that. I think greed is healthy. You can be greedy and still feel good about yourself." This statement from Ivan F. Boesky, made during his 1985 commencement address to the School of Business Administration of the University of California, Berkeley, was greeted with laughter and applause! That's right — agreement with and admiration for the chief perpetrator of what was at that time the biggest insider-trading scandal on Wall Street.

In referring to such unethical practices in the past, we used words like *wrong*. Today, we substitute nicer terms.

Meg Greenfield, in one of her *Newsweek* columns several years ago, very perceptively identified five new ways of thinking about wrong. To elaborate on her labels:

Right and Dumb

This term is used with openers such as, "I just can't believe he did that; it was so dumb. Surely, he knew he would be caught when..." Watergate, the Kettering Five scandal, the savings and loan debacles, the congressional check-kiting scandal, the Tail-Hook episode — all serve as good (or bad) examples. Journalists explain to us not that the behavior of those involved was morally wrong, but that they handled things badly.

Right and Not Necessarily Unconstitutional

This term has a flip-flop meaning that implies since the wrong was not mentioned specifically in the Constitution or the Bible, it is morally acceptable. As in, "What do you mean, I can't do that? Where in the Bible does it say . . . ?"

As an example of this reasoning, consider the corporate take-over game. Corporate raiders destroy equity, jobs, and communities. All for their own gain. Legitimate takeovers may serve some good. Corporate raiders do not.

We're forever writing our representatives in Congress to legislate against things that are "right" but unconstitutional, which would never have even entered the minds of our forebears back when they still had *wrong* in their vocabulary.

Right and Sick

This term is used for wrong behavior that is now considered a kind of mental or physical ailment, such as alcoholism, pedophilia, or the urge to rape. The "sick" person then has no personal, moral responsibility to control the behavior. As in, "I just can't help myself; I need your understanding and patience."

Have you considered the implications of the drunk-driving campaigns being shown on TV? The pitch is, if you're really a good friend, why would you let your drunk buddy crawl behind the wheel of a car? Why don't you take his keys away? While we would all agree that drunks shouldn't be on the road, since when has the responsibility for the behavior shifted from the would-be drunk to his friend? "Right and sick" has boiled down to, "He was under such pressure..."

Right and Only to Be Expected

As in, "Well, she asked for it. Why in the world would she leave the money in an unlocked desk drawer?" Does opportunity make the thief?

About rape assaults: "Well, why would she be on the street alone so late at night? She should have expected it." With that kind of reasoning, I'd have been guilty had I ever been attacked when I did my grocery shopping at midnight after my university classes.

We have turned victims into perpetrators of wrong and the guilty into opportunists.

Right and Complex

This term probably substitutes most often in the corporate setting, although we hear it, too, in official government explanations. As in, "Yes, normally, we hesitate to engage in that sort of thing, but there are extenuating circumstances here. The situation is very complex."

Whatever happened to wrong?

Frankly, for most of us, the term *wrong* involves too much effort of the will. According to Oscar Wilde, "The only way to get rid of temptation is to yield to it." Oh, it doesn't take much to say no when we're praying in church or meeting with Christian friends and associates. Eschewed reasoning usually strikes us when we're in the middle of a merger meeting, filling out expense reports, or designing direct-mail pieces.

On any given day in any given business, several of the following dilemmas will land on employee desks. Be prepared for them.

- Misrepresentations in reporting
- Misleading claims on products or services
- Price fixing
- Playing "memory loss" on prior commitments
- Setting policy that will create moral dilemmas for those who must implement that policy
- Badmouthing one's own company while spending the paycheck
- Passing on gossip
- Failing to speak up about unethical practices
- Failing to do something about safety hazards
- Failing to address discrimination
- Stepping on others to get ahead
- Giving misleading information about a competitor's product, service, or position
- Lying by silence
- Soliciting volunteer work or funds under false pretenses
- Wasting time on the job

• Taking an employer's supplies, inventory, or equipment for personal use

Some of us pray for help with our moral choices and then rush into morally questionable situations. The result is much like stuffing ourselves with high-calorie junk foods and then praying we don't gain weight.

Therefore, the time and place for a proper perspective on the moral boundaries is *before* we see the figures on the business plan, *before* we talk to the lawyer about the foggy new clause to be inserted, and *before* we hear what the competitor has planned.

True temptation is when we have opportunity and our will is all that restrains us. Ask not: Is it legal? Is it defensible? Is it understandable? Is it difficult? Is it complex? Is it to be expected under the circumstances? Is it politically correct? Instead, ask: Is it morally responsible? Is it morally right? Is it simply stupid and *wrong?*

For Further Reflection:

Finally, brethren, whatever things are true, whatever things are noble, whatever things are just, whatever things are pure, whatever things are lovely, whatever things are of good report, if there is any virtue and if there is anything praiseworthy—meditate on these things. (Phil. 4:8)

The Work Ethic Versus the Workaholic

For even when we were with you, we commanded you this:
If anyone will not work, neither shall he eat.

(2 Thess. 3:10)

It is in vain that you rise up early and go late to rest,
eating the bread of anxious toil; for he gives sleep
to his beloved.

(Ps. 127:2 NRSV)

We generally find people hold two extreme attitudes about work. First, there are those who think of it as Adam's curse, a grind, drudgery, something unpleasant stuck between the weekends. But nevertheless, as a necessary part of their right to live and get their fair share, they work to provide for themselves and their families.

Then there is the second attitude about work — those who love their work and find a great sense of fulfillment in it. In their minds, man was put on earth to achieve. They have found true happiness and true freedom in being able to do work they love and to make an adequate living doing it.

Workaholics come from both camps. Some are compelled by the work ethic and a sense of a curse, doom, and duty. Others are motivated by love of the work itself.

A few years ago workaholism was in favor and often dismissed with a wink. Magazines and newspapers frequently carried checklists to tell you if you were becoming a workaholic. If you "failed" the test and proved to be a borderline or full-fledged workaholic, you came away feeling good about yourself. You were going beyond the call of duty; you were committed; you were a superachiever.

Today, most of us are still working long hours, even if begrudgingly. In her book, *The Overworked American,* Juliet Schor, a Harvard economist, charts the expanding American work week over the past twenty years. According to her research, the average American employee now works 163 more hours per year than in 1970. Yes, Japanese factory workers put in even six more weeks' worth of hours, but they do it in a six-day work week and with few vacation days.

The question is, do we work such long hours by choice? If so, what about ourselves leads us to that choice?

I began to rethink my ideas about work a few years ago after a long walk with my parents. On one of their visits to my home, we were all strolling along under the tall pines at dusk when my parents began to reminisce about my childhood. After we'd gone through the days of my brother and me working in the cotton fields and my usual weekly household chores, we began to talk finances. My dad remarked, "We sure didn't have any money back then. I couldn't send you to college, and I didn't teach you much. But I guess the one thing your mother and I taught you was to work." Then he smiled but said with a very serious look in his eye, "The thing is, I think you learned that lesson too well."

You see, I'd just been advised that I needed to have major surgery right away, surgery that would require a long recuperation time. I had decided that I must put it off because I simply didn't have time. I had travel and speaking engagements, the seminar business, two books under contract, Christmas coming up, and the family. You get the picture.

The Bible never intended it to be so. God rested. He commanded us to rest. I began to give my attitude and what was happening in my life more serious thought. If a little work is good, isn't more work better?

No. For several reasons.

First, we soon find that the six days God gave us to do our work isn't enough. We scramble to squeeze a little more onto the agenda, and it spills over into Sunday. You know, the little things: reading professional journals and other job-related materials, balancing the checkbooks, paying the bills, buying the groceries, painting the spare bedroom. And the first thing you know, we're breaking God's commandment to keep His day holy.

Second, we find that our work crowds God's work out. We find less and less time to worship, to minister to others, to spend in personal Bible study and prayer. Nothing is so revealing about my prayer life as the dates entered in my little black prayer book — and the dates *not* entered there.

Third, work begins to crowd out the family. You miss more dinners together. You attend fewer worship services together. You talk less. The Apostle Paul insisted that the man who doesn't take care of his own family is worse than the heathen. Many of us interpret that care almost exclusively in terms of finances, so we stay at the office longer and work harder. But how about taking care of our family's emotional needs — their need of our time, attention, communication, presence, energy, and sensitivity?

Fourth, work begins to crowd out friends and makes us a very limited, unbalanced, and often boring person. When was the last time you went out to dinner with someone not associated with you through your work? When was the last time you had a serious conversation about new ideas, new trends, the world, art or literature or music, about spiritual matters?

Fifth, overwork can build hostility among your colleagues on the job. Do your colleagues slip in later than you do or go home earlier, leaving you breathing fire down the hall about their lack of commitment or accomplishment? The workaholic has little or no patience with others who don't work as long and as hard as he or she does. In fact, the workaholic even works harder to make up for others' "lack of commitment." Most employees can't follow the workaholic's long hours; therefore, the workaholic breeds hostility and antagonism when used as a standard for performance.

The sixth problem with workaholics is that their own performance slips. Don't confuse high energy levels and long hours with results. Samuel Butler observes, "To do great work a man must be very idle as well as very industrious." Just as a machine gets less efficient as its parts wear out, so the workaholic gets less efficient without rest and refueling. When was the last time you simply cleared your mind of work and let it float free?

The moments I savor most are often those spent on an airplane trip home after I've worked long hours on a client assignment. On those trips, when I'm too tired to do anything constructive, I give myself permission to let my mind roam unfocused. That's also the time I need the most notepaper at hand for the creative ideas that strike out of the blue.

When was the last time you had a completely new, exciting idea, one that gave you food for thought for as many pleasurable hours as a good book?

Finally, workaholics may be working to cover up emotional pain and problems that need to be dealt with rather than submerged in the job. If work is a medicine, it's often not the most effective cure. It's like taking an aspirin for fever without getting an antibiotic to kill the infection. Sooner or later the real disease will surface and take its toll on your job, your family, or your own mental well-being.

Work is good, right, and God's plan for our lives. Too much work is not better; it's harmful to all concerned. Are you reading this book at midnight or 5:00 A.M.? Why?

For Further Reflection:

She watches over the ways of her household,
And does not eat the bread of idleness. (Prov. 31:27)

And to the man he said, "Because you have listened to
the voice of your wife, and have eaten of the tree about
which I commanded you, 'You shall not eat of it,' cursed
is the ground because of you; in toil you shall eat of it
all the days of your life." (Gen. 3:17 NRSV)

Time Management and Creation of the Six-Day Workweek

Let all things be done decently and in order.
(1 Cor. 14:40)

So teach us to number our days,
That we may gain a heart of wisdom.
(Ps. 90:12)

Do you ever feel like standing up from your desk in the middle of the afternoon, blowing a loud whistle, and shouting "Freeze"? Unfortunately, the command wouldn't help because there's no such thing as a real time out. If you lose your money, you can start over to accumulate it. If you lose your health, you can often be healed or accommodated. If you forget things, you can relearn them. If you lose friends, you can apologize and restore them or make new ones. If you lose your good reputation, you can rebuild it by contriteness and effort. Many of God's gifts, such as grace, mercy, and love, are continuous.

Only time is limited; you can never recapture or rebuild it. But most of us lack a healthy respect for time—for its benefits or for its losses. In fact, we sometimes have a vague concept even of its passing. Have you ever noticed that when your favorite team is winning, a two-hour game seems but a couple of minutes? And when you're mowing the grass, two minutes drag by like two hours?

Respect for time and a true perspective of its value can be powerful motivators for redeeming the time that remains — as long as we stop whining about the lack of it and stop wasting it.

Several years ago when I thought myself too busy to exercise, a CEO of a locally headquartered corporation asked me to write a book for him. In the course of our writing project, I was forced to give up the idea that I was too busy to exercise when I heard his own exercise schedule: three lunch hours a week at the local club, a late-night hour of tennis twice a week, a Saturday morning of horseback riding or golf. Plus, he is an active deacon in his church, spends time at the Star of Hope Mission he helped found, and enjoys time with his active wife, children, and grandchildren. There went my exercise excuses, along with the notion that executives don't have adequate time for the important things in life.

National Liberty Corporation, which owns several insurance companies and affiliated marketing and service organizations nationwide, had as its chairman-founder Arthur S. DeMoss until his death in 1979. He was a pioneer in the mass marketing of life and health insurance and earned a prominent place in the history of insurance in this country. Arthur DeMoss had this to say about the management of time after his spiritual conversion (*God's Secrets of Success*, 1980, page 67):

In my own experience, the matter of time had been even more pressing than the money problem. It seemed that eighty hours a week were not sufficient even for the needs of the business, let alone finding time for Christian activity. Again I want to testify to the glory of God that the more time I have given Him the more He has given me in return. Now He has permitted and privileged me to spend almost as much time on His business as I used to devote to my own.

Charles H. Spurgeon agreed about the foolishness of mismanaging time: "He who rushes from his bed to his business without first spending time with God is as foolish as though he had not washed or dressed, and as unwise as one dashing to battle without arms or armor."

If you need a checklist to determine how well you manage your time, try this one:

- Are you becoming more forgetful lately? Do you forget to return telephone calls? To keep appointments, or even to set them? To buy gifts or send cards or notes for birthdays and anniversaries?
- Do you lose things easily—your keys, your checkbook, your favorite tie or scarf?
- Do you have a cluttered desk? Things out of place and tasks half-finished indicate a cluttered mind and cluttered time.
- Do you find yourself doing trivial, nonproductive things, such as considering a new color ink

for your memo pads? Such things are often desperate attempts to "at least get something done."

- Are you at odds with your coworkers, your friends, and your family? Are they nagging you about missing their deadlines, about not doing the report right, about not spending enough time with them?

- Has your time alone with God in prayer and Bible study become negotiable? Maybe you do, and maybe you don't?

- Do you have a free-floating sour attitude about your job, yourself, and the world in general? When we don't feel as though we're accomplishing something of value and enjoying the quality of our lives, we tend to blame others, ourselves, time, and circumstances.

Maybe you see the symptoms of mismanaged time in your life. What should you do? As with other things, follow Jesus' example. Like us, He was frequently interrupted on the job. He had the sick stop Him in the street and ask for healing. He had close friends call on Him in time of grief and ask for comfort and His physical presence. Just as we have new employees to train, He had disciples to question and teach. His time, like ours, was not always His own.

But He managed. He spent time with His family and friends at their important occasions, He spent time alone with God, and He accomplished His mission on earth.

So how did He do it? First, with preparation. He spent thirty years of His life preparing for the last three, and He never quit preparing. Even the week of His death, He still sent His disciples ahead to find His transportation and to prepare the upper room for His last lesson to them. How could He afford not to prepare for important occasions such as these?

Preparation. How much time do we spend going off half-cocked and then cleaning up the mess? How much time do we spend redoing projects because we didn't gather our resources and prepare things correctly the first time around?

How much time do we spend repairing damaged relationships because we didn't prepare before plunging? Have we assumed a certain friend was "strong enough" to take our well-meant advice, only to find that our comments have destroyed the friend's self-confidence? With a little preparation toward intimacy, the friend may have been able to profit from the advice.

Second, focus. Jesus focused on what was important and what was within range of His mission. He didn't spend much time collecting worldly possessions, but He spent a lot of time with those who stopped Him for physical and spiritual healing. Many modern-day businesses have learned the hard way about going off into unrelated product or service lines and losing the focus on their primary business.

Without focus, our minds and our businesses will self-destruct. How much time do we spend arranging and attending meetings that have little to do with real progress or results? How much time do we spend doing second-, third-, and fourth-priority items while our number-one priority is waiting in a holding pattern? How many days, weeks, or months do we drift through without ever setting clear goals for our accomplishments?

Third, delegation. Jesus delegated the less important chores. Do you remember that the Twelve picked up the leftover baskets of bread and fish on the hillside? Many of us can't delegate because we haven't done the first two things—prepare and focus. That is, we haven't taught and prepared our subordinates to do the quality work we expect. And we haven't focused on our mission far enough ahead to know what needs to be done and when it needs to be done to reach our goal.

If the Scripture teaches us anything about time, it teaches accountability. Take a good accounting of the wasted time around your office during the next few days. Someone has said that killing time is not murder; it's suicide.

For Further Reflection:

> Those who till their land will have plenty of food, but those who follow worthless pursuits have no sense. (Prov. 12:11 NRSV)

> A child who gathers in summer is prudent, but a child who sleeps in harvest brings shame. (Prov. 10:5 NRSV)

> See then that you walk circumspectly, not as fools but as wise, redeeming the time, because the days are evil. Therefore do not be unwise, but understand what the will of the Lord is. (Eph. 5:15–17)

The Craze to Advertise Ourselves

Finally, beloved, whatever is true, whatever is honorable, whatever is just, whatever is pure, whatever is pleasing, whatever is commendable, if there is any excellence and if there is anything worthy of praise, think about these things.
(Phil. 4:8 NRSV)

Only in our society could the refusal to advertise ourselves be considered arrogance. An actor who doesn't want to tour to promote his movie gets a shove from the producers and a thumbed nose from the general public. We seem to be saying, "Just who do you think you are? You're not *that* well known that you can take our accolades and our money for granted."

Joey Adams points out the difference between a civilian and an actor: When the civilian's house burns down, he calls his insurance agent; when an actor's house burns down, he calls his press agent.

Not only has the promotional craze washed over the stars and starlets, but it has also splashed over into the corporate scene:

- "Lose from six to thirty inches the first day." (Did someone double dare them to make that promise?)

- "Another of our best-selling authors brings you . . ." (Did you ever wonder how they could all be best-sellers and still be virtually unheard of by the general public?)
- "You can finance this dream vacation for only pennies a day . . ." (Does a thousand pennies a day for the next million years sound like a dream to you?)

I'm not about to insist advertising is unbiblical, or that your business stop advertising its products or services. In fact, we as Christians need to do more in advertising our faith and lifting Jesus up so He can draw people to Himself. Instead, I'm attempting to reconcile the biblical admonitions toward humility and this craze to advertise ourselves.

And to advertise deceptively, at that! Retailers often have three sets of sales figures for their newest product: the numbers they give the public, the numbers they really sold, and the numbers they give to the IRS.

Philippians 4:8 would be a good place to start when we meet with our PR staff. Is it true? Is your advertising completely, utterly, wholly true? "Best-selling" compared to what measure? The "largest" in what way? Can your claims be verified? By whom? What are you *not* telling the consumer and why?

When companies first began to offer gifts to prospects for listening to their spiel, I received a phone call from a solicitor wanting my husband and me to attend a seminar on vacation time-shares. The conversation went like this:

"Just for attending the one-hour seminar, you'll receive a free Lay-Z-Boy rocker."

"Just for listening? Even if we don't buy?"

"Just for listening. We figure your drive over and your time are worth that price."

"What kind of rocker did you say?"

"A Lay-Z-Boy rocker."

"Are you talking about the real Lay-Z-Boy, the brand name?"

"Yes, ma'am. A blue Lay-Z-Boy rocker valued at $288."

I took the bait. After the seminar, we received our "Lay-Z-Boy" — canvas fabric buttoned onto a wooden frame. Suitable for sitting on the beach, if the wind doesn't blow it over. Valued, I presume, at $2.88.

Is it honorable? Does your advertisement encourage people to their benefit? If questioned, would you like your name to be linked to the slogan, photo, or campaign? Would you be willing to go on television and accept responsibility for how this product changed an individual's lifestyle or benefited society as a whole?

Is it just? Does it leave the true impression about your competitors? Would you like your competitors to use the same tactics against you? Are your ads asking the age-old question, "Have you stopped beating your wife?"

Is it pure? In your own way, are you using sex to sell soap? Are your ads blatantly vulgar and immoral? Will your ads lead the consumer toward or away from a godly life?

With those stringent questions, how would you ever advertise anything successfully?

Try honesty and directness. How do you respond to a direct mail letter that begins, "Would you like to make a million dollars in the next six months?" Throw it away? So do most people, as I've found from questioning them in sales-writing workshops. And if somehow readers get tricked into reading to the bottom of page two ("So all you have to do is send us $99.95, and we'll send you our cassette tape telling you how to make your million dollars"), they get angry. They feel baited or "had." Few people respond well to that kind of come-on.

Don't underestimate the value of being forthright with your advertising message.

Isaac Newton said of his own accomplishments: "I do not know what I may appear to the world; but to myself I seem to have been only a boy playing on the seashore, and diverting myself in now and then finding a smoother pebble or a prettier shell than ordinary, whilst the great ocean of truth lay all undiscovered before me."

Quality work speaks for itself. Customers and colleagues often make the best and most effective references for our prospective clients and bosses.

When I was beginning my own consulting practice, I once heard a nationally known and highly regarded management consultant respond to a question from the audience about how he promoted himself and got so well known. His answer: "I hide, and they always seem to find me somehow."

Before advertising yourself, your product, or your service, check the previous list once again: Is it true? Is it just? Is it honorable? Is it pure?

The old saying that if we build a better mousetrap everyone will beat a path to our door is, of course, not always true. But I do think it's true more often than we businesspeople think. At the very least, shouldn't we as Christians make sure our mousetrap advertising is clear and honorable?

For Further Reflection:

Let another man praise you, and not your own mouth;
A stranger, and not your own lips. (Prov. 27:2)

But the meek shall inherit the land, and delight themselves in abundant prosperity. (Ps. 37:11 NRSV)

The reward for humility and fear of the LORD is riches and honor and life. (Prov. 22:4 NRSV)

For I say, through the grace given to me, to everyone who is among you, not to think of himself more highly than he ought to think, but to think soberly, as God has dealt to each one a measure of faith. (Rom. 12:3)

Advisers with a Bigger Briefcase and a Long-Distance Phone Number

Without counsel, plans go awry,
But in the multitude of counselors they are established.
(Prov. 15:22)

When Harry Truman assumed the presidency at the death of Roosevelt, Speaker of the House Sam Rayburn let Truman in on a little secret: "From here on out you're going to have lots of people around you. They'll try to put a wall around you and cut you off from any ideas but theirs. They'll tell you what a great man you are, Harry. But you and I both know you ain't" *(Bits and Pieces)*.

Even with a blow like that to the jaw of pride, few businesspeople would deny their need for good, sound advice. In his book *Think and Grow Rich,* Dr. Napoleon Hill tells us that Thomas Edison, Henry Ford, and Harvey Firestone were all close friends who consulted one another, often going off on retreats together to share ideas and develop solutions to problems. If these great minds needed advice, what about the rest of us?

But need doesn't motivate us all. "Many a man wins glory for prudence by seeking advice, then seeking advice as to what advice would be best to take, and finally following appetite," observed American physician Austin O'Malley. And according to eighteenth-century wit Samuel Johnson, "Advice is seldom welcome. Those who need it most like it least."

Those two short observations just about cover all the problems inherent with advice. We often have our minds made up before we seek advice. We get too many opinions, and then we don't know which to follow. When we really need advice, we don't like what we hear.

Let's look more closely at the first — having our minds made up before we seek advice. King Jehoshaphat of Judah (2 Chronicles 18) suffered from that malady. When King Ahab of Israel asked him to make an alliance and go to war against the Syrians and recapture their city of Ramoth Gilead, Jehoshaphat gave his answer before asking God what He thought of the idea! In effect he said to King Ahab, "My men are your men. Let's go. Oh, by the way, maybe we'd better call in some counselors and check with the Lord." When he didn't get the answer he wanted from God's prophet Micaiah, Ahab threw Micaiah in prison and went to battle anyway, and to his death.

Check yourself: How often do you really only want praise under the guise of advice?

"What do you think about this proposal?" you ask a colleague.

"Looks good," the friend answers. "But there are a couple of issues not addressed here. You might want to consider mentioning the heavy equipment the contractor will need for the job."

Your smile fades into a frown, you reclaim the proposal and lumber off to your office, convinced that your colleague is jealous because he didn't reel in the client.

Sometimes we don't reject the advice because it's too difficult or not what we want to hear, but because it's too simple, too obvious. Such was the case with Naaman, the commander-in-chief of the Syrian army, who sought a cure for his leprosy (2 Kings 5). He thought he had a big problem on his hands. He took the trouble to get a letter of introduction from his king and load himself with plenty of gifts and went with great fanfare to the king of Israel for healing by the prophet Elisha. Elisha didn't get too excited about his arrival; he merely sent a messenger out to tell Naaman to go wash himself in the Jordan River seven times to be healed.

Was Naaman thrilled that the solution was so easy? No. His response was to stalk away angrily. It was only when his own servants reasoned with him that he had a change of heart. "If the prophet had told you to do something very difficult, wouldn't you have done it?" they asked. "So what's your hang-up, simply because the advice is so easy to take?" Finally persuaded, Naaman followed the advice and was healed.

Almost all of us from time to time succumb to the urge to call in an adviser with a bigger briefcase and a long distance phone number. But why call in a consultant when your secretary gives you a plausible explanation and feasible solution? The proper mind-set for advice is an open mind—even when the advice sounds simple.

We recently hired an administrative assistant who within two days gave us a simple solution to a problem that had been plaguing us for years: how to keep track of our employees when they were traveling around the country. We thought the answer might be an office manager through which all messages were funneled, a big elaborate in-and-out board by the door, a new configuration of the phone system near the receptionist's work area. The new administrative assistant came up with a desktop system that cost us nothing and solved the travel and message issue immediately.

Don't overlook the answer at your fingertips.

The second problem with advice, as we mentioned earlier, is getting too many opinions or getting them from the wrong people. Most of the advice we get is largely our own; people know only as much about the situation as we've told them, and we almost always let them know the answer we want. Beware of those who feed you back your own advice and always echo the majority opinion.

Somehow we gravitate toward the people who don't know any more about the issues than we do. Although Proverbs 14:7 cautions us not to take advice from fools, fools don't always go around wearing tags identifying themselves as such. A good screening question to an adviser might be the cynic's query: "If you're so smart, why ain't you rich?" To what extent has the adviser taken his own advice and proven it to be accurate, appropriate, or effective?

As a consultant, speaker, and trainer, I can't tell you how much advice I have received on marketing my services:

- "The best way to get a client is still eyeball to eyeball."
- "The telephone is by far the most cost-effective sales method."
- "Direct-mail is the only way to go. Just tailor your stuff."
- "Network at industry meetings. You'll get the biggest payoff by far with that effort."
- "Do trade shows — you have to let people see your name out there with the big guys. You have to create awareness."
- "Never waste your money on trade shows. You can't afford to pay for 'awareness.' Your advertising dollars have to result in direct sales."

Coming from my state of total ignorance, my only hope in sorting through the advice was to make some logical deductions. I looked at each advice-giver's success with his or her recommended strategy.

Consider the Old Testament account of Rehoboam and his young friends (2 Chronicles 10). After King Solomon's death, his young, inexperienced son Rehoboam was crowned. As early as his inauguration, he was forced into a decision-making mode. The citizens came to him complaining of what a hard taskmaster his father had been. Just how did he intend to reign over them? What was his philosophy of government? So new King Rehoboam first went to his older, more experienced advisers. "They'll serve you faithfully the rest of your life," they advised, "if you treat them well."

But Rehoboam refused their advice and went to his young buddies. "Treat them rough and show them who's boss," they advised. Rehoboam had no more than gotten his philosophy stated over the loudspeaker when all but one tribe of his would-be kingdom deserted him.

There's no virtue in asking for a lot of advice from people who know no more than you. Is it pride that inhibits us from seeking out those brighter and more successful than we are and tapping the benefits of their experience?

Finally, in seeking out many counselors, we often hear from the people who have something personal at stake in our decision. Ahab found that out the hard way (1 Kings 21). When he complained to his wife, Jezebel, that his real estate deal with Naboth was on hold, Jezebel told him she knew just what to do. Not to worry, she assured him, and she arranged to have Naboth killed and then presented her husband with the property Naboth had refused to sell. We can only imagine that it wasn't purely unselfish love for her husband that created such passion to arrange the land deal!

The best advisers are those who, in addition to being wiser than we are, have no stake in the outcome. They have no horn of their own to blow, no career path to chart, no pocketbook to line.

What kind of advisers to choose? Not "yes" men and women. And not necessarily our friends and peers. But rather those wiser than ourselves, who share our ultimate values, who have no hope of personal profit from our decisions.

To keep from getting your own advice, be specific about the kind of advice you want. Do you want new ideas and alternatives that you haven't considered? Do you want additional information from the adviser? Do you want insight into how to think through or analyze the facts you have? Finally, stifle the urge to react too quickly, but rather, ponder what you hear.

Of course, there's still the biggest problem with advice: hearing advice we don't want. As others have noted, if at first you don't succeed, you'll get a lot of advice.

We often denigrate such "unsolicited" advice. Most of us react to advice that puts us in a bad light or goes against our desires just as King Amaziah did (2 Chronicles 25): "Since when have I asked your advice?" We would do better to follow King David's example: Although David committed grave wrongs, when the prophet Nathan came — unsolicited — to reveal them to him, he listened and repented of his ways.

To paraphrase the proverbs: There is safety in wise counselors who feel free to give us the best advice — whether it's what we want to hear or not.

For Further Reflection:

Where there is no counsel, the people fall;
But in the multitude of counselors there is safety.
(Prov. 11:14)

Listen to counsel and receive instruction,
That you may be wise in your latter days. (Prov. 19:20)

Someone's thoughts may be as deep as the ocean, but if
you are smart, you will discover them. (Prov. 20:5 CEV)

Too much pride causes trouble.
Be sensible and take advice. (Prov. 13:10 CEV)

The way of a fool is right in his own eyes,
But he who heeds counsel is wise. (Prov. 12:15)

Poverty and shame will come to him who
disdains correction,
But he who regards a rebuke will be honored.
(Prov. 13:18)

The ear that heeds wholesome admonition will
lodge among the wise.
Those who ignore instruction despise themselves,
but those who heed admonition gain understanding.
(Prov. 15:31–32 NRSV)

Stay away from fools, or you won't learn a thing.
(Prov. 14:7 CEV)

Affairs of State — and of the Office

> You have heard that it was said to those of old,
> "You shall not commit adultery." But I say to you that
> whoever looks at a woman to lust for her has already
> committed adultery with her in his heart.
>
> (Matt. 5:27–28)

"Sex has become one of the most discussed subjects of modern times," observed American Catholic Bishop Fulton J. Sheen. "The Victorians pretended it did not exist; the moderns pretend that nothing else exists."

Think how far we've come in our perspective on extramarital affairs. Just a few years ago, rumors and admissions of adultery ended one politician's race for the presidency. Now, when such stories surface, the only question in the public's mind seems to be, "What does adultery have to do with a person's ability to run the government?"

Corporations, fortunately, have a less tolerant view of their employees' affairs. Sexual interest and office affairs are not hidden for long. Someone who is not in the chain of command suddenly begins to show up at meetings beside the higher-ranking lover, knowing nothing about the meeting topic and caring less. Suddenly someone is personally hand-delivering all his or her reports, memos, or telephone messages. Someone is staying later and later after hours. Someone with an open-door policy suddenly has it closed too often.

Do companies care? If we are to believe all the management publications and interviews, yes. Mortimer R. Feinberg, chairman of BFS Psychological Associates of New York, and Aaron Levenstein, retired professor at Baruch College, surveyed a small sampling of managers to verify that impression. Out of their 112 respondents, seventy-six replied that people in their organizations had been asked by their bosses to "observe caution"; fifty managers said that warnings had been issued to discontinue the relationship; twelve reported that those involved in an affair had been denied a promotion; twenty managers reported that some action, including dismissal, had been taken because of the affair.

Why has management taken such a strong stand? Because of the legal headaches involved, for one thing. Corporations are hesitant to infringe on the personal lives of their employees, but at the same time they are held liable for sexual harassment on the job. The Senate hearings on Clarence Thomas focused a nation's attention on all the issues, misunderstandings, and potential for damage rooted in situations where men and women work together. To understate the case, sexual harassment deserves management's attention.

How different is the situation when the issue is not harassment, but mutual interest by the two people involved? As far as management is concerned, not much.

Walking the line between knowing of an affair and not knowing of an affair is rather difficult and can be quite costly in court.

Corporations are also concerned about the work performance and productivity of the individuals involved. If an adulterous affair leads to a family break-up, the employee's performance usually slips. Additionally, how much work time is spent in flirtatious chitchat on the phone and in secretly meeting the other party during the workday?

Third, management is concerned about the leaking of confidences from one department or situation to another via secrets shared lover to lover.

Additionally, there are cries of favoritism and petty jealousies when one is promoted or allowed special privileges because of the rank of the other person in the relationship. An employee having an affair creates tension and puts pressure on his morally upright co-workers. They see him or her getting away with things (for a time) and begin to think they are missing out, that perhaps their own straight theology, philosophy, and moral codes are incorrect. The conflict and contention intensify.

It's easy to see why management disapproves of office affairs.

Sometimes it's *not* so easy for the involved individuals themselves to see the dangers, both physical and spiritual, waiting to befall them. It's such an easy path to follow: from a distant look and acknowledgment of an attractive appearance; to open, flirtatious conversations;

to private, serious heart-to-heart talks that involve the emotions; to physical involvement.

The Bible gives us warning signs all along the way: admonitions about chaste appearance, warnings about idle and flirtatious chatter, commands to communicate our emotional needs only to our spouse, and advice to flee from sexual sin.

During my travels across the country for the past twelve years, I've had occasion to see and hear the various commitments — or lack of them — spouses have to each other. Two such displays come to mind: In the airport after an industry meeting, a colleague asked me to have a cup of coffee with him and discuss a marketing issue. We visited in the coffee shop for an hour. On the plane ride home, he managed to sit beside me. When the conversation grew a little uncomfortable for me, I steered our discussion toward his wife's part in his success. "She's brain-dead," he demurred.

Shocked, I apologized for my insensitivity.

"No," he said, "I just mean that she has nothing to do with what I do. I outgrew her a long time ago." With that comment, he put the final touches on an unattractive self-portrait.

The second incident came on the heels of a four-day training session. On the elevator, a man from the audience complimented me and then said, "I've phoned my wife every night this week to share with her what you've been teaching us. She's not working now — she plans to stay home with our kids until they enter school. But I don't want her to miss anything that I get to enjoy. We spend hours together on the phone, and this week has been no exception. You've shown us so much about..." But my mind trailed off for the rest of his compliment. His obvious love and commitment to his wife radiated a warm glow.

Whatever the intention at the beginning, whatever the commitment to a spouse up front, whatever the "line," the principal reason for interest in sex outside marriage is the loss of a higher faith and purpose. To fill the emptiness in one's life, an individual may look for fulfillment through physical pleasure and emotional excitement—the thrill of illicit emotional involvement and sex.

For those who would argue "Ours is not a casual thing. We care deeply for each other," the biblical warning is still the same. Eventually the guilt, the abandonment of God's blessings, and our shattered testimony destroy us.

"But I'm like the psalmist David, who was involved with Bathsheba," say others. "I still love the Lord, even though I've fallen to temptation." The primary fallacy with that claim and analogy is that they overlook repentance. King David's acknowledgment of sin did not stop with remorse and depression. He followed through with repentance, which can be defined only as obedience. He made things right.

Yes, God may "know our heart," but our heart's condition is revealed in our conduct, and our conduct is 95 percent of our testimony to others on the job. La Rochefoucauld reminds us, "It is much easier to suppress a first desire than to satisfy those that follow."

For Further Reflection:

Flee sexual immorality. Every sin that a man does is outside the body, but he who commits sexual immorality sins against his own body. (1 Cor. 6:18)

No temptation has overtaken you except such as is common to man; but God is faithful, who will not allow you to be tempted beyond what you are able, but with the temptation will also make the way of escape, that you may be able to bear it. (1 Cor. 10:13)

Beloved, I beg you as sojourners and pilgrims, abstain from fleshly lusts which war against the soul.
(1 Peter 2:11)

You should be faithful to your wife, just as you take water from your own well.
And don't be like a stream
from which just any woman may take a drink.
Save yourself for your wife and don't have sex with other women.
Be happy with the wife you married when you were young.
She is beautiful and graceful, just like a deer; you should be attracted to her and stay deeply in love.
Don't go crazy over a woman who is unfaithful to her own husband!
The LORD sees everything, and he watches us closely.
Sinners are trapped and caught by their own evil deeds.
They get lost and die because of their foolishness and lack of self-control. (Prov. 5:15–23 CEV)

God wants you to be holy, so don't be immoral in matters of sex. Respect and honor your wife. Don't be a slave of your desires or live like people who don't know God. You must not cheat any of the Lord's followers in matters of sex. Remember, we warned you that he punishes everyone who does such things. God didn't choose you to be filthy, but to be pure. (1 Thess. 4:3–7 CEV)

Letting the Lips Fall Where They May

Do not hasten in your spirit to be angry,
For anger rests in the bosom of fools.
(Eccl. 7:9)

Keep what you know to yourself, and you will be safe;
talk too much, and you are done for.
(Prov. 13:3 CEV)

Let all bitterness, wrath, anger, clamor, and evil speaking
be put away from you, with all malice.
(Eph. 4:31)

It's smart to be patient, but it's stupid to lose your temper.
(Prov. 14:29 CEV)

Will Rogers once observed, "People who fly into a rage always make a bad landing." Anger on the job causes mistakes, leads people to jump to wrong conclusions, saps productive energy and morale, creates untold conflict between employees and departments, and destroys a Christian witness.

"Well, that's just the way I am and just the way we run things. If you can't accept it, that's your problem." This sentiment is one we hear quite often from people who have something about them that others find offensive — especially when they don't want to accept responsibility for changing.

An older acquaintance of my family used to fly into a rage when his wife would "let him" miss the exit he wanted to take from the freeway. He cursed and slapped at the map and mumbled about his wife's worthlessness for hours after each such incident.

Some people speak of a bad temper as if it were a curse they have to learn to live with, much like being born left-handed or having size-10 feet.

Not so. Why would God tell us to control our anger if control weren't a reasonable possibility? The only kind of anger we're permitted is anger against sin. (When was the last time you saw anyone pitch a fit about someone's sin?)

Yet, we hold on to our "right" to get angry about lesser matters. In fact, a hot temper is a useful tool for many individuals on the job. Others feed angry colleagues whatever they want, much like they feed roaring lions at the zoo. Secretaries quickly interrupt themselves to find their angry boss's missing management reports. Subordinates nod agreement to their belligerent manager's schedule, knowing they can't meet the promised deadlines. Service reps quickly return a call to the yelling customer who insulted the receptionist.

Accompanying the same earlier-mentioned acquaintance to a jewelry store to buy his niece a necklace, I watched him unload on the clerk behind the counter.

"What do you mean you don't have the necklace in stock? It's in your catalog!"

"Yes, sir. It is in the annual catalog, but we're temporarily out of stock on that particular stone."

"You sorry . . ." and the curses flew again. A crowd gathered to watch, and I tried to inconspicuously disappear into its edges. But the tirade worked for him. He had three clerks and a manager hustling to try to make amends.

In addition to being a tool used to make others jump at our command, anger often is used to cover up for a lack of intelligence or poor performance. When someone in a meeting pounces on our inadequate investigation of a problem or on our weak conclusions, we often react with anger as a defense. The more put out we act with their "unreasonableness," the bigger cover we hope to spread over our own heads.

One of our seminar leaders felt the sting of a participant's frustration over his own lack of skills. At the first break of the seminar, the participant made it a point to tell the leader that she was the worst presenter he'd ever seen, totally unclear and totally unfamiliar with her information. (Never mind that this instructor averages a 9.8 rating on a 10-point scale.) She apologized that what she'd said had not met his needs and that she had been unclear. At the end of the seminar, he finished unloading by writing on his course evaluation: "Your suits are too big on you — they just hang. You wear the wrong colors. You need to learn to speak clearly."

Our instructor was devastated by the personal attack, until the participant's supervisor reviewed all the course evaluations. The supervisor added insight about this attendee's own weak job performance and fear of being dismissed for lack of the skills he was supposed to be learning in the seminar.

Some people excel in using anger as a screen.

When people are wrong and can't admit it, they get angry; when they're right, it's incredible how calm they can be.

The Bible speaks of several expressions of anger: cursing; jumping to the worst conclusions about people; complaining; giving smart-aleck retorts; and being argumentative, oversensitive, and bitter. These symptoms we don't need a checklist to uncover; they are usually readily apparent to all those around.

So how do we eliminate those overt signs of anger in our own conduct and attitude? Admit your anger, talk the problem through with those involved, and then ask God to remove it from your mind.

We *don't* get rid of anger by trying to bury it inside. The English poet William Blake penned this truth:

> I was angry with my friend;
> I told my wrath, my wrath did end.
> I was angry with my foe;
> I told it not, my wrath did grow.

An old Chinese proverb further warns: "The fire you kindle for your enemy often burns yourself more than him." Anger that we talk through in a calm way usually leads us to forgiveness, reconciliation, and strength. The anger that we try to ignore or bury most often hardens into bitterness and a desire for revenge.

A bad temper distorts our perceptions and business judgments and makes us appear immature, undisciplined, and lacking in reason. An angry man makes those colleagues and customers who observe his outbursts his superiors.

For Further Reflection:

But I say to you that whoever is angry with his brother without a cause shall be in danger of the judgment. (Matt. 5:22)

Losing your temper is foolish; ignoring an insult is smart. (Prov. 12:16 CEV)

A quick-tempered man acts foolishly,
And a man of wicked intentions is hated. (Prov. 14:17)

The discretion of a man makes him slow to anger,
And his glory is to overlook a transgression.
(Prov. 19:11)

Do you see a man hasty in his words?
There is more hope for a fool than for him. (Prov. 29:20)

Don't be a fool and quickly lose your temper — be sensible and patient. (Prov. 29:11 CEV)

An angry man stirs up strife,
And a furious man abounds in transgression.
(Prov. 29:22)

Those who are hot-tempered stir up strife, but those who
are slow to anger calm contention. (Prov. 15:18 NRSV)

But now you yourselves are to put off all these: anger,
wrath, malice, blasphemy, filthy language out of your
mouth. (Col. 3:8)

"Be angry and do not sin": do not let the sun go down
on your wrath. (Eph. 4:26)

Appraising on Performance
or Appearance

Do not withhold good from those to whom it is due,
When it is in the power of your hand to do so.
(Prov. 3:27)

Don't depend on things like fancy hairdos or gold jewelry
or expensive clothes to make you look beautiful. Be
beautiful in your heart by being gentle and quiet.
(1 Peter 3:3–4 CEV)

For as he thinks in his heart, so is he.
(Prov. 23:7)

Researchers tell us that attractive people have an edge
with first impressions. They are often thought to be
brighter, smarter, more capable, and more personable
than their unattractive colleagues. Since these research
findings were first published, the media have continued
to bombard us with how-to's on making that all-important
impression on the boss or client.

The dress-for-success people tell us what color, what
fabric, and what style to wear. Public relation firms
emphasize the value of an appropriate company name,
charging $35,000-$50,000 to rename us and give us a
fresh start. Career consultants remind us to circulate

semiannual memos to our boss and colleagues that highlight our accomplishments on the job. Even politicians
have joined the appearance-is-everything bandwagon,
being coached on proper gestures and makeup for television appearances. Historians observe that for want of
a good makeup artist, Richard Nixon lost the 1960 elec-
tion during his four debates with Kennedy.

Even outward behavior suggestive of underlying motives can be deceiving. You will recall the Acts 5 story
of early church members Ananias and Sapphira, who
generously sold some of their property to donate the
proceeds to the church. Theirs was a good deed — almost.
The problem was that they wanted their friends to think
they were more generous than they really were. They
reported to the church a selling price far lower than what
they actually received and pocketed the difference. The
Holy Spirit struck them dead for their deception.

Behavior, although usually more revealing than appearance, may still present inaccuracies about one's true
colors. With our limited discernment of others' motives,
we can be fooled by the good done by someone with
wrong motives; we can be equally deceived by the harm
done by someone with the right motives and proper skills.

Nevertheless, supervisors must judge the outward
performance of those they supervise, and colleagues
often pass along opinions about their peers. Whether
those judgments come formally in written performance
appraisals or informally through oral praise or criticism,
we should be careful to consider the whole person and
the whole performance.

We almost lost a very good employee because of our misjudgment based on outward appearances. A newly hired administrative assistant had difficulty in taking initiative and making decisions on even the smallest matters. At the outset, when she would report every minute detail of a situation to her boss and ask for his decision, the boss would get irritated. Then he began to make comments about her skills in other areas. "Don't give that invoice to Carol to verify; she won't be able to calculate it." "Don't ask Carol; she wouldn't know where to look in the files to find that." "We can't depend on Carol to handle that — that requires attention to detail." All were conclusions that did not logically follow from her lack of initiative.

Finally, at the point of terminating her employment, her boss began to dump situations back into her lap. "Carol, get the facts and then do whatever you think is best."

And she did. As she grew in the job, she learned to take initiative when her boss was traveling and to handle clients with finesse. At the end of a year, she had become one of our most dedicated, knowledgeable employees.

Personnel directors who specialize in training managers to conduct performance appraisals and review those appraisals often observe and warn against the "halo" and "pitchfork" tendencies. A supervisor who thinks someone is likable tends to rate that individual high in all performance areas. If the supervisor does not particularly like the employee or finds one or two objectionable traits or skill weaknesses, she tends to downgrade the employee in all areas.

And some employees, quite polished in handling themselves well before their superiors, manage to dash up the corporate ladder simply because they're able to outrun the problems they create in each job before they're promoted to the next one.

Not only do inaccurate labels about weak performance do serious wrong, we often err with the mediocre to good labels. We cheat employees and ourselves by not recognizing the potential in those who consistently perform well without advertising themselves through the trappings of appearance.

Several years ago I had occasion to work with a large industrial and educational film producer on a video series and its accompanying workbooks. In all my years of writing, I have never worked with a more capable, conscientious editor than on that project. Clearly knowledgeable on every grammatical matter we discussed, he did not have to ask the whys and wherefores of editorial changes I wanted. Every suggestion and correction was made willingly and scrupulously. An outsider would have thought his name was going on the screen and the book cover.

After concluding the project, I commented on the editor's expertise to a vice-president of the company, who responded: "Wayne? You don't say! Well, he's such a quiet guy. Minds his own business. I didn't know he was that kind of an employee. Maybe we should consider his capabilities for some other projects we're into."

Why not, indeed? Supervisors may get so caught up in the appearance-is-everything mode that they overlook their best workers.

We should continually monitor our own reaction to others:

- Do we selfishly hold our good employees back from deserved promotions simply because we don't want to lose them and don't want the hassle of training others to replace them?
- Do we let our own personality likes and dislikes color our judgments about work performance?
- Do we use our appraisals as opportunities to praise a job well done, as well as to point out areas needing improvement?
- Do we suggest and provide further training, experience, or education for the future benefit of the employee?

"For as he thinks in his heart, so is he" (Prov. 23:7). That verse applies equally to the supervised and the supervisor.

For Further Reflection:

Do not be a witness against your neighbor without cause,
and do not deceive with your lips.
Do not say, "I will do to others as they have done to me;
I will pay them back for what they have done."
(Prov. 24:28–29 NRSV)

Let no evil talk come out of your mouths, but only what is useful for building up, as there is need, so that your words may give grace to those who hear.
(Eph. 4:29 NRSV)

Boredom — or the Boardroom Blues

The backslider gets bored with himself;
the godly man's life is exciting.
(Prov. 14:14 TLB)

But I say to you that for every idle word men may speak,
they will give account of it in the day of judgment.
(Matt. 12:36)

Many people consider boredom a mark of sophistication. They think it's plebeian to show wonder at or enthusiasm for almost any idea, event, or hopeful prospect. In fact, many of our movie idols and great writers have adopted cynicism as their worldview and gain satisfaction when media reviewers of their work comment on their perceptiveness about the human condition. You may have noticed the same pretense of cynicism or "sophistication" in colleagues who never laugh at anyone else's witticisms and who never join in anyone else's excitement. In other words, they pride themselves in not getting too excited about anything in life.

Murmuring and griping, in addition to a pretense of sophistication, are other causes for boredom. "The habit of thinking ill of everything and everyone is tiresome to ourselves and to all around us," Pope John XXIII once remarked. A constant disposition of irritability and complaining makes any circumstance unhappy and meaningless for us.

However, a complaining disposition or attempts at sophistication are not the primary causes of boredom for the majority of us. The matter is much simpler or, depending on your perspective, more complex.

"A yawn may be defined as a silent yell," observes essayist and critic Gilbert Keith Chesterton. That yell may be one of anger and protest that life hasn't dealt with us properly. Or it may be a scream that we ourselves don't even hear—a cry from the shallowness of our lives for something more meaningful to which to devote our days.

In fact, we become bored in direct proportion to our loss of interest in people and pursuits higher than ourselves. The biggest booster of boredom is selfishness. The more we indulge ourselves, the more we demand. Therefore, the more selfish we are, the more bored we get. Show me a person who dines every night on his favorite foods, who lives in a dream house, who can write a check for anything he wants, who has the ability to perform any necessary job skill, who calls any person his friend, and who is recognized by everybody in the marketplace, and I'll show you a very bored individual.

Bebe Moore Campbell, writing in *Savvy* magazine several years ago, described her own descent from commitment to burnout and boredom. She still vividly remembered the woman standing in front of her church pleading for volunteers to "pattern" her retarded child.

Bebe persuaded three fourteen-year-old friends to join her each day in their efforts to move the limbs of this retarded child in the hope of helping her learn to crawl someday.

In college, she tutored a young boy with poor reading skills. She passed out petitions and marched to end the war in Vietnam. She met for endless hours to organize and pressure school administrators into admitting more black students and hiring black faculty.

As a young adult, she wrote letters to prisoners and became a "big sister" for two children.

Bebe recited her earlier commitments to underscore who she had become. Her commitment is no longer to hands-on help. Now, if she does anything at all, she merely writes a letter or sends a check. She admitted becoming lulled by self-centeredness, complacency, and abundance. The original flower child now dresses for success and has it her way at Burger King.

How about you? Do you ever look out the car window and see the street people scrounging for food? See the spaced-out teen wandering around the mall? See the unmarried pregnant teen with a cynical sneer and a cigarette hanging from her lip? Hear the neighbor drive the car through the garage wall and then shout at his family for nagging him about drunk driving? Observe the lonely eyes of the divorced mother alone at Christmastime without her children? See a college student shuffling across the parking lot with no place to go during the holidays? Read Position Wanted ads in the newspapers? Remember the elderly aunt in the nursing home?

Sitting dog-tired on the subway or in your car during rush-hour traffic after another long, boring day, do you ever look around you and think *Somebody ought to do something* about all those needs?

Only a mission higher than ourselves can extinguish boredom and ignite excitement in our lives. As near as your phone, there's an agency, an organization, or a church waiting for your call.

For Further Reflection:

And whatever you do, do it heartily, as to the Lord and not to men. (Col. 3:23)

Corporate Compassion

Caring for the poor is lending to the LORD,
and you will be well repaid.
(Prov. 19:17 CEV)

Thus says the LORD of hosts:
"Execute true justice,
Show mercy and compassion
Everyone to his brother."
(Zech. 7:9)

But when you give alms, do not let your left hand
know what your right hand is doing,
so that your alms may be done in secret;
and your Father who sees in secret will reward you.
(Matt. 6:3–4 NRSV)

Americans donated $122 billion in 1990 to charitable organizations. U.S. companies donated approximately $5.9 billion of that amount. Yet, when newspaper headlines tell of mismanagement and excessive staff salaries at national or local charities, some corporations and individuals alike use that as an excuse to turn an unconcerned glance toward the needy and go back to the computer, business as usual.

Another line of reasoning that helps some businesspeople turn a cold shoulder to need is the "pull one's self up by the bootstraps" philosophy. Former HEW Secretary John W. Gardner, writing in *Newsweek*, refused to brush the poverty problem away so easily: "For every talent poverty has stimulated, it has blighted a hundred."

For every businessperson who claims that most of every dollar on charity and compassion is wasted, there are thousands who disagree. We've all heard of the Ronald McDonald Houses that shelter families of hospitalized children receiving extended medical treatment. In fact, the Ronald McDonald's Children's Charities, set up in McDonald's founder Ray Kroc's memory after his death in 1984, have also contributed millions to other groups helping children.

Other philanthropic efforts by organizations such as the Gannett Foundation and B. Dalton Bookseller have been undertaken to help those millions of illiterate adults who can't read the front page of a newspaper, the warning on a can of poison, or a sign that says, IN CASE OF EMERGENCY, PUSH THIS BUTTON.

Corporate Angel Network (CAN) was the compassionate idea of a former cancer patient and licensed pilot, Priscilla Blum. She had noticed that numerous corporate airplanes flew in and out of the airport every day with empty seats. Why not see if they would fly cancer patients free to their distant medical treatments whenever they made routine business flights? The idea was not without problems because corporate flight schedules were sporadic and often canceled.

Guidepost magazine tells the story of how, upon one such cancellation, the Norton Simon company chairman phoned CAN to apologize and wanted to know what he could do personally to help these victims. A staff member suggested he write a letter to his colleagues in other corporations and ask for their help. As a result, 100 other corporations signed up to transport patients through this nonprofit organization in White Plains, New York.

The list is almost endless for corporations who want to reach out to those in need:

- *Medical programs* — Red Cross blood bank drives, medical research projects, CPR training, and wellness campaigns.
- *Educational assistance* — Summer work programs, scholarships, speakers, equipment donations to local schools.
- *Youth programs* — Assistance to disadvantaged community youth in the form of scholarships, camps, shelters, recreational centers, tutoring programs.
- *Fund-raising drives* — Donations and publicity to encourage support of local charities.
- *Counseling programs* — Help for alcohol and drug abuse, marital and family problems, financial and retirement planning.

But, you may be thinking, corporations can *afford* to have compassion for the problems of the world. They do it for publicity, for tax deductions, even for profit. Before you write off all such efforts to motives of self-interest, consider the *individuals* who often initiate or become involved in such projects.

Carla Weaver, profiled in a *Houston Chronicle* story several years ago, held a corporate planning manager's job with Pennzoil and dreamed of feeding the poor with nutritious, inexpensive soybean meals. Carla wrote and had approved a corporate policy that granted a leave of absence for employees involved in charitable activities.

Then she left her fast-track job and went to Costa Rica, dipped into her savings to set up a small factory with four employees, and ordered 17,000 pounds of soybeans and several tons of rice and macaroni. She has sold the nutritious, inexpensive, easy-to-prepare food to the public school systems and many companies with employee cafeterias and hopes to market it to other underdeveloped countries in Central America and around the world. Although any such business has to be profitable to operate, her drive was compassion as she followed a Costa Rican friend and minister around the country.

Then there's Carl Umland, retired from Exxon Chemicals. He joined the Christian organization Habitat for Humanity to construct new homes to sell at cost, financed by interest-free loans for the poor. The houses are built primarily by volunteer labor using donated supplies. All the money received goes back into building more houses. Those who purchase the houses must volunteer 500 hours of labor, either to build their own home or someone else's. Habitat for Humanity International has built or refurbished more than 13,000 homes, half in the U.S. and half in foreign countries. This volunteer labor is their practical expression of their faith and God's command about helping "the least of these." Former president Jimmy Carter has also donated days and weeks to this effort.

In Hilton Head, South Carolina, an anonymous benefactor has changed the lives of more than 60 youngsters. In 1992, he set up an educational program to help eighth-graders. Through the program administrator, Susan Barnwell, he proposed to pay for a tutoring program — including director, office, computers, books — to support and counsel kids who needed help in school. For those who wanted to go to college or technical school, he offered to pay their tuition. Already, those students who have improved their grades have collected $30,000 in scholarship certificates.

Employers who encourage their own employees to get involved in such corporate philanthropic activities boost morale tremendously. Employees appreciate the opportunity to be involved in something beyond themselves and their own self-interests — whether the project be collecting toys for Christmas, distributing food at Thanksgiving, or repainting homes for the elderly.

Lester A. Picker, writing in *Your Company* magazine (Winter 1992), suggests that both large and small corporations consider any or all of the following ways to give:

- *Time* — Volunteer time for small projects or for service on boards and committees.

- *Services or facilities* — Offer your service or product free of charge to a nonprofit group. Or, if your facility and equipment sit idle at times, permit nonprofits to use them.
- *Depreciated property* — Donate your old furniture or equipment to nonprofits. They can then save their cash for programs.
- *Excess inventory* — Donate old product lines.
- *Revenue* — Offer to give a certain percentage of revenues on certain product lines. Or team up with a nonprofit that wants to market your product or service. Let the nonprofit take the profit.
- *Cash* — Give money and ask for accountability for its use.

But just because you're not a CEO or decision maker with authority to grant gifts from the corporate coffers, don't overlook your individual charitable opportunities.

Consider other ways that a compassionate heart contributes to the world. Thoughtfulness, sensitivity, and kindness are often worth much more than money. In fact, when we compare good and evil in the world, much of the difference between the two can be labeled compassion.

Although we have little hesitation in categorizing as evil the acts of a murderer, a rapist, a terrorist, or a drug dealer, we often fail to see the lack of compassion in the everyday acts or nonacts around us.

A lack of compassion may simply mean looking "through" a coworker in need of attention. Have you ever noticed how your colleagues lay aside paper and pen, clutch pocketbooks, and putter toward the elevators at lunchtime, leaving one person unnoticed and uninvited? Or how, in a meeting, when ideas are forthcoming and massaged with yeas and nays, one timidly offered idea fetches not a word, a glance, or a second thought and serves its giver as a reminder of the isolation enforced by an insensitive group.

Again and again, the New Testament tells us that Jesus looked at the multitudes with compassion. But it often cost Him time, effort, and popularity. Are we willing, as corporations or as individuals, to do the same?

Never will we be more Christlike than in our moments of compassion.

For Further Reflection:

He who despises his neighbor sins;
But he who has mercy on the poor, happy is he.
(Prov. 14:21)

Finally, all of you be of one mind, having compassion for one another; love as brothers, be tenderhearted, be courteous. (1 Peter 3:8)

Conflict with Coworkers: The Paul and Barnabas Battle

If it is possible, as much as depends on you, live peaceably
with all men. Beloved, do not avenge yourselves,
but rather give place to wrath; for it is written,
"Vengeance is Mine, I will repay," says the Lord.
(Rom. 12:18–19)

Do all things without complaining and disputing,
that you may become blameless and harmless, children
of God without fault in the midst of a crooked and perverse
generation, among whom you shine as lights in the world.
(Phil. 2:14–15)

One of the most frustrating experiences in human relationships is when we learn another person doesn't share our viewpoints, expectations, needs, or values. Perhaps we take a look at the long-range problems, and others see only the short-term benefits. Maybe we thrive on risk, and others value security. We may push thoroughness, and others may preach speed.

You'll note that the Apostle Paul didn't admonish us never to express our differences. Instead, he says, "if at all possible" live in peace with all men. We can work out or give in to conflicts over schedules, wants, needs, or goals. Only those conflicts of value are unavoidable.

A few years back a friend of mine had no choice but to resign his job over one such value conflict. As manager of a major discount store, he was put in the awkward position of having to deal with the nationwide chain's fraudulent practice against various manufacturers who advertised through discount coupons. The practice was for the store personnel themselves to take off all the discount coupons attached to the merchandise, which were meant for the consumer, and mail those coupons back to the manufacturer for the rebates.

Senior management of the discount chain justified its action by explaining that the consumer wasn't hurt in any way. The store simply reduced the price of the item by the amount of the discount and passed on the savings. The result was that this chain could always advertise the lowest prices and undersell the competition. My manager friend faced a conflict of values with the senior management over this practice and had to quit his job.

But conflicts of wants, needs, and expectations don't always demand such drastic action. Such conflicts *can* be resolved and deserve at least our best efforts.

Furthermore, conflict isn't something we should necessarily be ashamed of, because conflict can lead to better decisions and problem solving. Such was the case with the conflict between the Greeks and the Hebrews over the daily distribution of food to the widows among them (Acts 6). As a result of the conflict being brought out in the open and discussed, the church selected seven deacons to carry on the daily administrative work.

Conflict can also be a benefit when it stretches us intellectually and emotionally. When someone challenges our ideas or actions, we have to review and reevaluate them to be able to defend them. If we discover that we can't defend them, then we're better off to discard them. Peter decided that was the case when confronted about the Gospel being for Gentiles as well as for Jews (Acts 10).

So how do we go about making conflict positive rather than negative on the job?

To begin with, as soon as we roll up our sleeves to resolve a conflict, we should try to wash our ego from our work. Have you ever noticed how we make introductions? "This is Harriet Hargrove, an accountant who works in our revenue section." Or, "This is Jack Bright, the engineer who designed this year's model virtually single-handedly." At work, we're known for our work. Therefore, when someone points out a disagreement or change or error, we often feel as though they are attacking us personally.

If we could only drain the ego from ourselves in much the same way that a mechanic lets the air out of a tire before repairing it, we probably wouldn't find disagreement so disagreeable.

With ego out of the way, we're ready to talk things over. Self-control is rarely more difficult than when discussing a disagreement. "A man without self-control is as defenseless as a city with broken-down walls" (Prov. 25:28 TLB). We can't possibly come up with a long-lasting, effective resolution to conflict until we have ourselves under control.

With self-control, it's much easier to treat the other person with respect and with basic good manners, both musts if we intend to make the resolution a lasting one. Manners are what separate the civilized from the barbarians. Manners restrain oneself, give preference to others, create order out of chaos, collect the educated and the uneducated into one profile, and march them toward the same goal. I would dare to say that more conflicts in the corporate world result from a simple lack of manners than from genuine needs or values.

In all conflict resolution, we must also be very careful not to wound another's self-esteem: "Well, if you had returned my phone call yesterday before we went into that meeting, rather than bumbling around in your usual daydream world . . ." Needless to say, this type of response does not induce people to return phone calls more promptly in the future. We should never attack the person, but rather should discuss only the action or behavior that needs changing.

Not: "Jill, I've told you several times about coming in late. That's simply irresponsible behavior. You get paid to be here to answer the phone, and you need to get yourself out of bed in time to be here at 8:00."

But: "Jill, several times we've discussed your coming to work late. Is there a continuing problem with being here at 8:00?"

"Yes, there is. My elderly mother has started calling me long-distance every morning and some mornings I just can't get her off the phone."

"I see. That can really be tough. But we have to have you here promptly at 8:00 each morning to cover the phones. Maybe you can ask your mother to call in the evenings, or to call you earlier in the morning. Whichever way you decide to handle the problem, we need you here no later than 8:00."

Deal with the behavior, not the character of the individual. Make every effort to leave self-esteem intact.

Finally, as we get around to stating our views and hearing those of our coworker, there's one last consideration. According to English essayist Joseph Addison: "If men would consider not so much wherein they differ, as wherein they agree, there would be far less of uncharitableness and angry feeling in the world."

Find areas of agreement before you launch into the deep of disagreement. Do you have the same profit goals? Do you both want to please the customer? Where do your facts, opinions, or goals match? That's the starting point for resolving differences.

If, after long discussion, you don't see your divergent positions coming together, remember that some differences may not need to be resolved. Both sides may be right, as early New Testament missionaries Paul and Barnabas discovered. Their conflict over whether to take young John Mark along with them eventually led to the same goals (Acts 15). Although John Mark hadn't been exactly what they'd needed on their first missionary journey, Barnabas believed in giving him a second chance. People need second chances; Barnabas was right.

But so was Paul. Perhaps he felt that time to spread the Gospel was short, that they didn't have time to waste on encouraging or training the younger, less committed workers. Paul and his future circumstances — prison, stonings, beatings — demanded nothing less than total commitment.

Two sides can be right. Paul and Barnabas accepted that, and each went his own way.

Supreme Court Justice William O. Douglas observed: "Today it is generally recognized that all corporations possess an element of public interest. A corporation director must think not only of the stockholder but also of the laborer, the supplier, the purchaser, and the ultimate consumer. Our economy is but a chain which can be no stronger than any one of its links. We all stand together or fall together in our highly industrialized society of today."

If we can keep this fragility in our minds as we discuss our work conflicts, resolutions might more often and more quickly tap us on the shoulder.

For Further Reflection:

A brother offended is harder to win than a strong city,
And contentions are like the bars of a castle.
(Prov. 18:19)

A fool's lips enter into contention,
And his mouth calls for blows. (Prov. 18:6)

It is honorable for a man to stop striving,
Since any fool can start a quarrel. (Prov. 20:3)

Fools start fights everywhere while wise men try to keep
peace. (Prov. 29:8 TLB)

Like somebody who takes a passing dog by the ears is
one who meddles in the quarrel of another. (Prov. 26:17
NRSV)

Let all bitterness, wrath, anger, clamor, and evil speaking
be put away from you, with all malice. (Eph. 4:31)

To him who strikes you on the one cheek, offer the other
also. And from him who takes away your cloak, do not
withhold your tunic either. (Luke 6:29)

Cooperation: The Mary and Martha Dilemma

If anyone wants to sue you and take away your tunic, let him
have your cloak also. And whoever compels you to go
one mile, go with him two. Give to him who asks you, and
from him who wants to borrow from you do not turn away.
(Matt. 5:40–42)

But Martha was distracted with much serving,
and she approached Him and said, "Lord, do
You not care that my sister has left me to serve alone?
Therefore tell her to help me."
(Luke 10:40)

I receive a call from the education coordinator at a
client's office, who is trying to ready things for our
next seminar. Could we immediately ship her twenty-
four books for the attendees? Someone from the purchasing department, she assures us, will get in touch in a few
days to give us the billing information. Sure. We send the
books.

A few weeks later, we phone the responsible person
in the purchasing department to ask about the paperwork.
She has no paperwork, knows nothing about the order,
and does not have time to check on it for us. Okay. So
we just wait.

Two days later, a second person in the purchasing department phones to order twenty-four books. We explain that the twenty-four books have already been sent. He insists that he doesn't know anything about the first twenty-four books but that his paperwork says for him to order twenty-four books. We mention the *high* probability that this is the same order we have already shipped. Can he please check that out? No, that's "not his department." We give in and accept the second order, shipping another twenty-four books and billing with the purchase order number he gives.

Three days later, the person calls back and says he has too many books. He accepts no blame, saying that the person who told us to ship the books in the first place "was out of line." Will we accept the returned books? Yes.

An hour later, we get a call from the education coordinator in another branch for another seminar. Will we send twenty books? We explain that the purchasing department has just called asking permission to return twenty-four books, and we suggest that they shuffle those books down the hall to her, rather than go to the trouble and expense and delay of returning them to us. Sure, she says, no problem.

The next day we get a call from the purchasing department, asking why we were billing for two shipments of twenty-four books. We give her all the details, including the names and phone numbers of her colleagues, and ask her to work out the problem. No, she insists, the education coordinators have no business phoning us themselves. No, she will not contact them to straighten out the mess. "Let them take care of it themselves."

I phone the education coordinator to verify that I indeed should send the extra books and not depend on the switch. How dare the purchasing department, she grumbles, mess things up! Would she take the other names and phone numbers from me so she can straighten out the problem? No, she refuses, it's the purchasing department's fault; let them contact her.

The next day . . . well, I won't bore you with the rest of the logjam. You can probably think of several similar incidents of your own. In fact, some people seem to think that such mix-ups are inevitable in large bureaucracies. Maybe they are. But you, on the other hand, can do your best to avoid them where your job and department are concerned.

What causes an uncooperative attitude? Stubbornness. Pride. Laziness. Jealousies — comparing your paycheck or workload or abilities to someone else's. Perhaps resentment, a sense of someone's not pulling his or her own weight, and the feeling of frustration in having to "pick up the slack."

Such was the case between Mary and Martha during Jesus' visit. Mary had chosen the better part of sitting at Jesus' feet. Martha permitted herself to feel like a martyr and to become resentful of the added responsibility of dinner guests when Mary felt no such responsibility and offered no help.

Some employers and bosses purposefully set up competitive situations that breed resentment and jealousy rather than cooperation. Harvard professor, author, and management consultant, Dr. Rosabeth Moss Kanter has dubbed these competitive environments "cowboy management."

Cowboy management makes competition, rather than cooperation, a virtue. Cowboy managers like to get out there in the wilderness with a few trusty pals and no company or government restraints. They practice survival of the fittest for their product, service, idea, or department. Kanter has conducted extensive research in trying to find if this kind of competition has been successful in the major corporations across the nation.

Success with this philosophy was rare. Kanter found that creating winners and losers within the corporation was bad strategy. In well-managed, successful organizations, the competition was a race against the clock or the task, not against other employees. In other words, in a successful sales campaign, reps battled to increase their own past sales volumes or to achieve a certain percentage increase in territories that did not overlap those of their colleagues.

In Kanter's words: "In every high-performing company I've seen—in my own research and consulting practice as well as in that of other researchers—cooperation was more effective than competition in fostering productivity and innovation."

Miller Business Systems, an office products firm located in the Dallas/Fort Worth metroplex, has used cooperation to improve its customer service department drastically. The employees there are divided into teams and each teammember is rewarded on the team's sales volume rather than on individual volume. Service for the customer has improved because no one shuns answering time-consuming questions in favor of taking the easy, large orders. In the past, before the team cooperative structure was implemented, turnover for the customer service department was the highest in the company. With the cooperative effort of a team reward system, morale has skyrocketed. Miller's has a waiting list of employees wanting to transfer into customer service, now a model department for the industry.

Another study reported in *Small Business Reports* shows similar results in day-to-day management decisions. Dr. John P. Kotter of the Harvard Business School observed the daily activities of fifteen successful top managers to discover their management style. He concluded that although senior managers occasionally exercised authority by issuing directives, they generally used subtle means of persuasion and tried to gain others' cooperation rather than demanding that they blindly follow orders against their will.

Management consultants and professors merely confirm what the Bible has told us all along about the human spirit: We cannot sincerely help other people without helping ourselves in the process. We gain spiritual benefit and nourishment from a cooperative, not a competitive, attitude.

Going the second mile is a testimony to our non-Christian colleagues. Our serving when we'd rather be sitting may be just what a colleague needs to refresh his or her spirit on the job. In doing so with the right attitude, we may in turn refresh our own spirits.

It's simply a value-added consideration that our corporations, as well as our people, run more successfully on cooperation than competition.

For Further Reflection:

> With all lowliness and gentleness, with longsuffering, bearing with one another in love, endeavoring to keep the unity of the Spirit in the bond of peace. (Eph. 4:2–3)

Corporate Courtesy

And just as you want men to do to you,
you also do to them likewise.
(Luke 6:31)

Love is kind and patient, never jealous, boastful, proud, or
rude. Love isn't selfish or quick tempered.
It doesn't keep a record of wrongs that others do.
(1 Cor. 13:4–5 CEV)

There's something about walking into a business office that makes otherwise courteous people shed their social mores and become barbarians. Why else would we have to put signs in the restroom that say, PLEASE DEPOSIT TOWELS IN THE WASTEBASKET and signs above the water fountain that say, FOR SANITARY PURPOSES, PLEASE DO NOT SPIT IN THIS FOUNTAIN? Is boorish behavior contagious?

Standing in line at a copier at the public library, I observed this incident. A woman, who was making copies from a pile of journal articles, noticed a man waiting impatiently behind her. She turned to him and explained that since she had so much copying to do she would stop for a moment to permit him to make a copy. He nodded, not too gratefully, and she stepped aside, whereupon the man literally took over the machine for multiple copies, keeping her waiting for quite some time to finish the chore she had so graciously interrupted for him.

For the traveling businessperson, rudeness is rampant on the road: in taxis, planes, restaurants, and hotels. At Washington's Dulles airport, I crawled into a taxi about midnight. When I gave the taxi driver the name of a nearby hotel, he began to curse me and his bad luck for getting all the short fares. For the entire four-minute ride, he cursed the whole U.S. government and economic system for exploiting foreigners.

The everyday insensitivities around all of us are endless: not returning phone calls, leaving spilled coffee on the snack room chair, leaving messages that no one can decipher, keeping other meeting attendees waiting while you do "just one more thing," looking through people who smile and speak in the halls.

Some people plead ignorance about such rudeness. A trainer at a major corporation asked to keep a software package we had demonstrated so that she could show it to others who had input to the buying decision. A week later, a sales rep called her, wanting to pick up the demo package to show another client; he left a complete message about the nature of his call.

When she did not return the call, the rep tried again. First, the trainer was "unavailable"; then she was "in a training session"; then she was "in a meeting"; then she was "out of the office for a few days." Five months later (yes, five!), the sales rep gave up trying to get her on the phone and wrote a letter explaining once again that he needed the demo package returned.

By overnight express, the sales rep got the package and an apology letter from the trainer explaining that she was "so sorry" she had forgotten she still had the package and would have returned the phone calls if she'd known that was why he was calling.

Wasn't the sales rep due an apology for the unreturned calls, regardless of his reason for calling?

Why do these discourtesies happen? Some see customers, callers, and colleagues as all alike — faceless people in a crowded sea of corporate competition. Our high-tech marketplace has fostered low-touch relationships.

But the fact that other people are insensitive or rude to us should not dictate our own response. Someone has said that a test of good manners is being able to put up pleasantly with bad ones. Good manners may require little sacrifice on our part — a little time, a little forethought, extra steps out of our way, extra strokes of the pen or keyboard.

A few months ago, I walked into a firm at five minutes before my scheduled appointment time. The receptionist, on the phone, never glanced up as I approached the desk. I waited. The receptionist took the second call after the first ended, still not glancing up. She took the third call just as the second ended, this time briefly scowling at me as if to say, "Can't you see I'm busy?"

After the third conversation, she dialed a call herself to present a delayed message to another employee. I slipped a business card in front of her and nodded toward her watch. The receptionist ignored both gestures and turned to answer a passing employee, who asked where Tom and Harold had gone for lunch. The receptionist picked up the fourth call, still having not acknowledged my presence in front of her desk. And the fifth call. Finally to the rescue, my appointment wandered out into the hallway, saw me, and motioned for me to join him in his office. Still no acknowledgment from the receptionist at the arrival or departure a half hour later.

At the Zig Ziglar corporation two days later, the experience was totally different. When I walked through the door, the receptionist rose to her feet. "And you must be Dianna Booher. Great. We're expecting you. I'd like you to meet ..." and she introduced me to the other two employees seated nearby. What a difference a small courtesy or two makes.

"Life is not so short but that there is always time for courtesy," insisted Ralph Waldo Emerson. Even as Christ hurried through the crowds on a busy day, He stopped when one believing woman touched the hem of His garment. He wasn't too busy to acknowledge her, even commenting on her faith and insight in coming to Him. No doubt Jesus delegated some of His ministry to His twelve assistants, but we have the same option. We, too, can have an assistant take or give a message or return a call or a kindness.

Courtesy is really a matter of sensitivity to others' needs and feelings. Author Jonathan Swift wisely observed, "Good manners is the art of making those people easy with whom we converse. Whoever makes the fewest people uneasy is the best bred in the company."

Recently I attended an informational meeting where we had two speakers, the vice-president of the company and the controller. The meeting attendees were middle managers who'd flown in from across the country for a briefing on a new budgeting procedure. The controller made her presentation about the whys and wherefores of the new budgeting procedures, using the most complex jargon possible and illustrating authorizations for expenditures in the millions of dollars.

After she finished, the vice-president called her to the side and made the following suggestion: "Before the next group comes in, why don't you plan to tone down the illustrations a little? These people don't have the authority to approve the kind of dollars you're talking about. Let's use figures that are a little more in line with their responsibilities. We don't want them to feel unimportant in the scheme of things."

From watching this VP shake hands and visit with his managers around the room, I got the distinct impression that he had the same sensitivity to others in all his dealings. Maybe your experience has been much the same as mine and the anonymous people who keep saying, "The bigger they are, the nicer they are." Courtesy is sensitivity.

But common courtesy is not all that common in corporate America. In fact, it has almost become a contradiction in terms. Why shouldn't courtesy become a cause for the Christian?

For Further Reflection:

A soft answer turns away wrath. (Prov. 15:1)

Don't be jealous or proud, but be humble and consider others more important than yourselves. Care about them as much as you care about yourselves. (Phil. 2:3–4 CEV)

Paying Your Debts When the Debits Say You Can't

Don't withhold repayment of your debts. Don't say
"some other time," if you can pay now.
(Prov. 3:27–28 TLB)

The rich rules over the poor,
And the borrower is servant to the lender.
(Prov. 22:7)

Can you imagine the size of the army the U.S. could
field if the government used soon-to-be King
David's recruiting method outlined in 1 Samuel 22:2?
His soldiers were debtors; they had few choices open to
them. With the typical American owing thousands of
dollars, a good many debtors feel enough desperation to
escape the burden by any means available—whether
that means joining a foreign guerrilla army or faking an
accident and beginning a new life under an assumed
name.

Although most would agree that many people are
living far beyond their means, many would also con-
demn themselves and these fellow undisciplined
souls who have gotten themselves into such a predic-
ament.

On the other hand, businesses often take a totally different perspective on the matter of paying their debts. They often rob Peter to pay Paul — or don't pay Paul at all.

Certainly if a business has a "net 30 days" agreement, it makes good business sense to keep the use of its money as long as possible. But what about those times when there's no such agreement, when businesses knowingly violate the trust of their creditors or even their employees?

A Houston manufacturing company employing over 500 people blew the whistle at 5:00 P.M. Friday, and then announced that it was filing for bankruptcy. None of the employees received their paychecks for the last two weeks' work, even though the company had decided to file for bankruptcy before the pay period began. In fact, they'd made an agreement with the bookkeeper that if she stayed on two extra weeks to wind things up, she'd get a paycheck and be the only employee not left holding the bag.

Most of us also have grown familiar with the "30-day stretch." Your payment is overdue and you make a phone call to ask its whereabouts. The accountant or other contact tells you, "Oh, I don't think we ever received that invoice. Would you drop us another copy in the mail?" Or, "We haven't received that in Accounting. Let me check on it and call you Monday." Or, "You know, I think the delay might be that we weren't sure we had your correct address so we've been trying to check that out."

And here's one that held up a $30,000 check owed us for over thirteen months: "We're converting our computer records and as soon as we can restore all our historical files, we'll have a correct record of how much we owe you."

A married college couple had similar difficulties with an employer. The husband worked for a Dallas roofer who frequently duped his employees out of their wages. As roofers, they were told to collect the tags off the bundles of shingles as they put each bundle on the houses during the work week. On the last workday of each week, they were supposed to turn in their tags to collect so many dollars per tag.

Quite frequently, the roofer refused to pay his employees (almost exclusively students working their way through college) the full amount he owed them, claiming that someone had "stolen" extra tags from other job sites and turned in too many. Therefore, he would summarily subtract a few tags, or $40–60, from each worker's weekly paycheck.

And on many paydays, he failed to show up at quitting time, sending word that he was "tied up" and his employees would have to catch him later for their money. The truth was that his employees often had to drop by the office four or five times before catching him several days later and getting their paychecks. That scenario was the contractor's way of managing his cash flow problem.

The problem does not stop with the business owner. Individuals, too, play loose with their debts.

Credit card holders run up exorbitant debts not for the necessities in life but for the extras—video cameras, weekend vacations, a new boat, or dining out. And when the monthly payments get too high, they declare bankruptcy and start over—at someone else's expense. Ask people who have gotten in over their heads with credit cards, and they'll tell you it has become a way of life. Have now, pay later.

Common practice? Yes. Ethical? No.

According to the government, one student in seven defaults on federal education loans. The rest of us taxpayers get stuck with paying the tab for their education.

Does being in debt make good sense—for the business or the individual?

Businesses and individuals under heavy debt lose their freedom. They often make decisions not according to preference but under pressure. Debtors lack the freedom to experiment with new ideas that might be risky but promising for the future.

Some companies and individuals despair of ever being able to pay off their debt and consequently give up the challenge. "Poverty is hard, but debt is horrible," observed evangelist Charles Spurgeon.

Not only does debt restrict freedom, but it also leads to compromise. In Luke 16 we read about the servant who scurried around to those who owed his master money and offered them the "opportunity" to repay only half of their total debt. Debt often leads sensible, honest people into compromises they would never make under ordinary circumstances.

Finally, debt can be an expression of our lack of faith in God to meet our needs adequately. Elisha commanded the widow to sell her remaining oil, pay her debt, and prepare to live on the rest (2 Kings 4:7). Some of us have refused to operate our businesses or live our lives on what God provides.

Debt destroys our testimony, usurps our freedom, causes us to compromise our convictions, and often makes poor business sense. Think about it the next time you're tempted to say "Charge it."

For Further Reflection:

The wicked borrow, and do not pay back, but the righteous are generous and keep giving. (Ps. 37:21 NRSV)

The violence of the wicked will destroy them, Because they refuse to do justice. (Prov. 21:7)

Then she came and told the man of God. And he said, "Go, sell the oil and pay your debt; and you and your sons live on the rest." (2 Kings 4:7)

Haman's Hang-ups About Enemies

Do not rejoice when your enemy falls,
And do not let your heart be glad when he stumbles.
(Prov. 24:17)

Don't try to get even.
Trust the LORD, and he will help you.
(Prov. 20:22 CEV)

When we please the LORD, even our enemies
make friends with us.
(Prov. 16:7 CEV)

When a man's ways please the LORD,
He makes even his enemies to be at peace with him.
(Prov. 16:7)

Will Rogers reportedly never met a man he didn't like, but he dared not speculate that all those he met *liked him!* All people who stand for certain values, causes, or ideas are bound to find those who oppose them. Even Jesus had enemies.

For most of us, it's not those enemies that plague us — those who dislike us because of our moral uprightness or the good we do. Instead, most of us create enemies unnecessarily. We make enemies because of our own stubbornness, lack of sensitivity, selfishness, unkindness, jealousy, or pride. Those are the kind of enemies we need to deal with on a more positive level.

In the book of Esther, we see how Haman creates his own enemy, Mordecai, because of pride and jealousy. When the Jew Mordecai refuses to bow down to Haman as the king's official, Haman grows perturbed enough to talk the king into signing a decree that all those Jews who practice such strange customs in their land and have allegiances other than to the king should be put to death. As time goes on, we see Haman's jealousy grow toward Mordecai.

First, the king orders Haman to parade through the streets, leading Mordecai dressed in the king's robe and riding the king's donkey as a reward for a long-forgotten good deed toward the king — a reward Haman thought he himself deserved. Twice Haman goes home to complain to his wife about the favor the king shows to Mordecai rather than to himself.

Finally, determined to put a stop to his perceived enemy, Haman has a gallows built on which he plans to have Mordecai hanged. But before Haman can get rid of his enemy, Mordecai talks his niece, Queen Esther, into intervening with the king on behalf of the Jewish people and saving them from Haman's plot of death. Together they thwart Haman's plans. The king is so outraged with Haman that he has him hanged on the gallows Haman had planned to use for his enemy, Mordecai.

If we learn anything from Haman's hanging, we learn how *not* to treat the enemies we create.

First, we learn that we can't ignore them. According to an Italian proverb: "Have you fifty friends? It is not enough. Have you one enemy? It is too much."

From various studies on customer service, we've learned that every dissatisfied customer tells ten to twelve people about the bad experience. Bad news spreads. As far as our own experience goes, it doesn't matter who's right or wrong in the situation. You still can't afford to ignore an enemy.

Several years ago, a client contracted with us to develop a custom training program, to teach the program to their corporate trainers in two workshops, and then to turn over rights of the program to their corporation. We included our daily rate for the workshops we were to teach in a line-by-line breakdown of the total investment.

We did the work; the client was extremely pleased. At the end of the second workshop we conducted for them, we turned the program over to their own trainers. About three months later, we received another call from our client contact: "Our own trainers haven't been able to do the course as well as your people did. We'd like you to continue to teach the course for us. Please give us a quote on your daily rate."

We quoted our new 10 percent higher fee that had gone into effect since we'd completed the project for the client. But to the client, it didn't matter that the old job was bid and delivered at the previous year's prices as we'd agreed. From his perspective, it was a "bait-and-switch" deal. He expected us to keep our prices the same for any work done for him at any time in the future.

We explained that the fee increase was the first in three years and had been announced for the past two months. But no explanation could change his belief that he'd been wronged. He decided that they would continue to do the best they could, teaching the course themselves.

As other prospective clients called us to ask about our doing similar custom projects for them, we continued to give the earlier contact as a reference. After all, he and his people did say they were pleased with the results of the training program. Only after the third prospective client deal turned suddenly sour did we discover that this one "enemy" wouldn't go away. In his mind, he had been wronged and he intended to spread the word.

What to do in such a situation? Gaining victory over an enemy should not be our goal. If we squelch our enemy for the moment, we have at best gained a little time for our own pursuits; we have not removed the cause or the ill will. Only when we reconcile the enemy—change his or her will or attitude about us—can we say we have dealt positively and safely with a person.

So how do we reconcile an enemy? First, we have to get rid of the impulse for revenge. Such was certainly not the case with Haman. When the king wanted to honor Mordecai for his earlier good deed in foiling an assassination plot, Haman certainly had the power to do good. The problem was that he hated being in that position! Unlike Haman, our own hearts have to be set for the cause of reconciliation rather than conflict. We have to want to turn the enemy into a friend.

The poet Longfellow once observed, "If we could read the secret history of our enemies, we should find in each man's life sorrow and suffering enough to disarm all hostility." Try to understand your enemy's viewpoint and motive, and with that understanding you will soften your own heart. The impulse to punish is powerful; only the love of God can drain that urge.

A second way Haman dealt with his self-created enemy was to cast doubt on him through half-truths. By alluding to the "strange" Jewish customs and their allegiance to God, Haman implied that the Jews would show disrespect to King Ahasuerus and do him harm.

It's still a favorite ploy of some people to use such half-truths to undo. In front of a group of coworkers, they ask questions like: "Have you finally completed the report that you had such difficulty understanding?" "Have you been able to stop so many of your good employees from wanting to transfer out of your department?" "Did you phone your senator opposing that bill, or do you favor taking advantage of the poor?"

In fact, questions of this nature posed on political subjects have been used to unfairly sabotage good men by forcing yes or no answers on complex issues. We would do well to avoid Haman's example of using half-truths to produce erroneous conclusions.

Another matter in dealing with enemies is to listen to them. That's right—listen to them. We should realize that our enemies may have a point about us. In fact, we may come much closer to the truth of our situation by examining our enemy's opinion rather than our own.

Finally, we must do unto our enemies as if they were our friends, just as we would have them treat us. Haman all too clearly learned the wisdom of that truth when the gallows meant for Mordecai became the instrument of his own death.

Shakespeare penned his own version of this biblical truth in a rather specific analogy: "Heat not a furnace for your foe so hot that it do singe yourself." Many businesspeople, I'm sure, could make similar analogies from past experience:

- "Set not the sales quota so high for your despised salesperson that the CEO chides you, the manager, for not reaching it."
- "Assign not all the unpopular, gruesome projects to one disliked employee so that she becomes discouraged and resigns, leaving you in a lurch."
- "Withhold not needed data from the report writer, or the vice-president will ask you to plan your next budget according to the report's erroneous information."
- "Devalue not the ideas of your coworker in department meetings so that when she becomes your supervisor you fear to make recommendations."

Taking care not to create enemies unnecessarily and reconciling those we have is often our stronger test of Christian maturity.

For Further Reflection:

If your enemy is hungry, give him bread to eat;
And if he is thirsty, give him water to drink;
For so you will heap coals of fire on his head,
And the LORD will reward you. (Prov. 25:21–22)

Do not say, "I will do to others as they have done to me;
I will pay them back for what they have done."
(Prov. 24:29 NRSV)

You have heard that it was said, "An eye for an eye and a tooth for a tooth." But I tell you not to resist an evil person. But whoever slaps you on your right cheek, turn the other to him also. If anyone wants to sue you and take away your tunic, let him have your cloak also. And whoever compels you to go one mile, go with him two. (Matt. 5:38–41)

A Stressed Conscience

But if you do not forgive, neither will your Father
in heaven forgive your trespasses.
(Mark 11:26)

Therefore if you bring your gift to the altar,
and there remember that your brother has something
against you, leave your gift there before the altar,
and go your way. First be reconciled to your brother,
and then come and offer your gift.
(Matt. 5:23–24)

A man's home is his castle, they say. Perhaps that's
true for many people because home is the only
place they can go to get out from under the pressure of a
stressed conscience and escape the feeling country-west-
ern writers so colorfully phrase as "being done wrong."

When I recently asked an acquaintance how she liked
her new job, she held her grim countenance and whis-
pered conspiratorially, "Let's go to lunch sometime."
Later in the day, I had occasion to be in the department
with her former colleagues, who happened to mention
her transfer:

"She got a really good job, but she has never liked it.
To keep from laying off people after the buyout and
reorganization, management decided to shuffle us all
around. Since Catherine had just finished her MBA, they

moved her to personnel. She could have been a real star there and set up the department just about any way she wanted it. But the thing was, she felt she had no choice. She couldn't understand why we all got to stay in this department and she was the only one to have to leave. She's never gotten over it. She's just miserable. We all used to get along so well; I just don't know why she thinks someone had it in for her."

According to Ephesians 4:31, the signs of a convicted conscience are anger, bitterness, and strife — whether we have been wronged or have wronged others.

A fellow church member shared with the congregation his conviction about a wrong done to his company. When he was transferred, he moved across the country with the understanding that his company would pay the moving expenses. But by the time he submitted all the expenses, the executive who'd made the promise had retired from the company. Result: The company would not reimburse him. The employee vowed at that point to make the company regret that decision; he'd get even.

And he did. Over the next few years, he stole thousands of dollars worth of tools and spare parts from the company warehouse, rationalizing that the company "owed it to him." He even rationalized with the Lord, telling himself that he had a "ministry" with the tools, because on weekends he repaired the cars of his family and friends without charge. One by one, these friends began to quit calling him for help. But again, he rationalized to himself that he could then spend more time with his family.

Finally, conviction fell on him so strongly that he had to load up his garage full of tools, write out a check to cover all the years' worth of spare parts, and confront his boss with the returned equipment and a confession.

The boss's response: "I don't think the company can afford to lose an employee who now has a clear conscience."

If you need a one-time checklist to verify a clear conscience, ask yourself this question: Is there someone in your past you would dread to meet on the street? The answer to that question will outline your course of action.

A clear conscience—both ours and the other person's—places demands on us, as employers and employees, in two ways. We must forgive, and we must be forgiven. A clear conscience is the ability to say we have made things right with every individual who has ever wronged us or whom we have ever wronged.

Several years ago, an individual came into my life who created much pain for our family. Because of petty jealousies, personal ambition, and plain insecurity, he created great economic and emotional upheaval for us. I harbored such bitterness toward this man that I avoided going to the shopping mall or out to dinner for fear of meeting him or his wife. When I occasionally saw him, I became physically ill, nauseated. But it finally dawned on me that the problem was mine; this man's pride probably would never allow him to ask forgiveness. Only after I wrote *him* a letter asking his forgiveness for my holding a grudge did I become free of the pain his behavior and decision had caused.

Excuses such as these do not let us off the hook: "But she was clearly in the wrong." "He doesn't even know about it." "It was such a minor issue." No matter the circumstances, you need a clear conscience about the relationship.

For starters in gaining forgiveness and a clear conscience, try this on-the-job checklist:

- Have I ever padded a resume?
- Have I ever gossiped about why someone left a job?
- Have I ever intentionally given the wrong impression about someone or some competitor's company by what I said or left unsaid?
- Have I ever taken credit for someone else's ideas or accomplishments, passing them off as my own?
- Have I ever pouted, complained, or wished evil for someone because of their promotion, bonus, or award?

Probably the biggest question is, "Have I ever refused to really forgive someone for hurting me in these same ways?" If so, rethink your position. The parable in Matthew 18 tells about the debtor who was forgiven a great debt when he pleaded for mercy, then had his fellowman thrown in prison for a paltry debt he couldn't pay.

By both asking and offering forgiveness, we rid ourselves of a stressed conscience. We gain emotional freedom, peace of mind, and God's forgiveness for our own errors as well. Begrudging forgiveness saps the joy out of an otherwise productive day. How can you lose by giving up a grudge?

For Further Reflection:

He who covers his sins will not prosper,
But whoever confesses and forsakes them will have mercy. (Prov. 28:13)

Bearing with one another, and forgiving one another, if anyone has a complaint against another; even as Christ forgave you, so you also must do. But above all these things put on love which is the bond of perfection. (Col. 3:13–14)

And forgive us our debts,
As we forgive our debtors. (Matt. 6:12)

Where Your Treasure Is: Stockholders and Sunday Morning Offerings

But this I say: He who sows sparingly will also reap sparingly, and he who sows bountifully will also reap bountifully. So let each one give as he purposes in his heart, not grudgingly or of necessity; for God loves a cheerful giver.
(2 Cor. 9:6–7)

Do not lay up for yourselves treasures on earth, where moth and rust destroy and where thieves break in and steal; but lay up for yourselves treasures in heaven, where neither moth nor rust destroys and where thieves do not break in and steal. For where your treasure is, there your heart will be also.
(Matt. 6:19–21)

Honour the LORD with your possessions,
And with the firstfruits of all your increase;
So your barns will be filled with plenty,
And your vats will overflow with new wine.
(Prov. 3:9–10)

What I gave, I have; what I spent, I had; what I kept, I lost. That old epitaph couldn't be more biblical and more appropriate for those of us in the business world.

The Bible has much to say about money. It doesn't refer just to what we give directly to God in our tithes and offerings, but also includes giving to advance His causes in the world while helping the needy along the way. The emphasis on money is well placed, and for good reason. The way we handle the money we earn determines how much of it we keep — eternally.

Promises of prosperity almost always follow the principles of giving. No matter how much we give away, God promises that we will still have all our physical needs met, that our children will not go hungry, and that we will know true contentment. Those promises come in pint-size or giant-size.

During early marriage while still in college, my husband and I struggled along on two part-time salaries, with few extras. One December we received eighty dollars in a Christmas card, with directions to buy gifts for our toddlers. But only hours before, I had spoken with a neighbor with a much more pressing need than ours that Christmas. Her husband had deserted her and their four children, leaving them destitute, and her electricity was about to be shut off for nonpayment. One of the greatest pleasures I've ever had was tucking that money into another envelope and sliding it under the neighbor's door before the 4:00 deadline given by the utility company.

But that wasn't the end of the story. I would have been satisfied if it had been, for all the pleasure I received from knowing for the very first time I'd met a real, desperate need in someone's life. In the week that followed, we received two more checks in the mail from loving church members—enough to buy Christmas presents, pay our next semester's tuition, and even have leftovers in the bank.

Through the years, there have been many such repayments from God to His givers. A husband lost his job after he and his wife had just pledged a large extra offering, above their regular tithe, to a church building program. Scared, yes, they were. But since God had tutored them all through the years about His giving principles, they continued their weekly pledges for the many months the husband was without steady work. During that first year, the wife's struggling business took off through no effort of her own, and the year's receipts were just under four times those of the previous year— abundantly more than enough to cover their extra pledge.

Stories such as these are all around us. Why aren't we all so trusting and generous in every situation and circumstance? That's what has led me to study the next question:

Why don't we *always* see prosperity immediately follow giving? Our problem may come with a defective attitude about the whole giving/prosperity cycle.

One such inappropriate attitude in giving is to think God can be bribed to provide success. A colleague of mine frequently comments about calling the nuns in a particular convent to pledge money for their current cause and to request their prayers for the success of one of his business ventures. On one of his latest deals, he asked God for success in exchange for a percentage of the profits.

On occasion, as the biblical writer noted, we tend to consider giving to God only when we're staring at red ink on the balance sheet. "God, if You'll just . . . then I promise that I'll give . . ." God isn't a broker, and He doesn't delight in such deals.

Another wrong attitude is giving to cover conscience. We pull some shady shenanigan to win a bid and clinch a deal, then try to salve our conscience by giving God half the profit. Or we feel a tug on our heart to share some time and attention with a down-in-the-mouth coworker, but our time is so limited; why not just write a check and pay somebody else to do good?

God is not interested in weighing our gifts on a scale according to our deeds. The Pharisees were ever so careful to tithe every tidbit of income, and rightly so, but Jesus assured them that monetary gifts didn't cover all the other matters they left undone. Giving is no substitute for obedience.

Still another faulty attitude is a begrudging spirit, whether giving to God or to others. We often hear this question about gifts to the church: "How *much* should I give?" What these people are usually asking is, "How *little* can I give and still win God's favor?" With regard to how much, we should recall that the Pharisees millions were not enough, but the widow's mite was more than enough.

Considering charity toward their fellowmen, some people begrudge giving so much that they hold all their money until the reading of their will. Someone once pointed out that the person who saves all his wealth until the time of his death only conveys to the world that he would have kept it to himself longer. Giving only when death leaves us no better alternative may be pride's desire to leave a monument to oneself. Such a gift can even be motivated by fear; the dying person may hope the large sum will wipe out the debt of an unrighteous life.

Another wrong attitude is giving to buy friends. Some of those close to the late rock singer Elvis Presley tell us that was his motivation for the impulsive giving of large gifts to total strangers. Cash-for-carry creates a multitude of charities at the marketplace door — some worthy, some not. As the proverb notes, givers have many friends; we have to have good sense in our giving, just as in every other decision.

So what is the right attitude about giving? Generosity and secrecy.

The English essayist Charles Lamb says, "The greatest pleasure I know is to do a good action by stealth, and to have it found out by accident." Have you ever wondered if the big bucks corporations give to charity and then use as the basis of an advertising campaign will be deducted on God's account of blessings?

To pity the poor is human; to alleviate their need is generosity; to do so secretly is Godlike.

Finally, we should have a grateful attitude about our ability to give. A businessman once confided to his pastor that it hadn't been so difficult to tithe when his check was only a hundred dollars a week. And it hadn't been too hard when he was making only a thousand a week. But, he lamented, with the kind of earnings he had at present, that 10 percent was an awfully big chunk. The pastor immediately knew how to solve his problem: "Then let's get on our knees and ask God if he can lower your salary back to what it was earlier."

Seneca observed: "This is the law of benefits between men; the one ought to forget at once what he has given, and the other ought never to forget what he has received."

Gratitude, not gain, is the proper motive for giving. We enjoy most those treasures and pleasures that we give away.

For Further Reflection:

"Bring all the tithes into the storehouse,
That there may be food in My house,
And try Me now in this,"
Says the LORD of hosts,
"If I will not open for you the windows of heaven
And pour out for you such blessing
That there will not be room enough to receive it."
(Mal. 3:10)

It is well with those who deal generously and lend, who conduct their affairs with justice.
For the righteous will never be moved; they will be remembered forever.
They are not afraid of evil tidings; their hearts are firm, secure in the LORD.
Their hearts are steady, they will not be afraid; in the end they will look in triumph on their foes.
They have distributed freely, they have given to the poor;

their righteousness endures forever; their horn is exalted
in honor. (Ps. 112:5–9 NRSV)

He who gives to the poor will not lack,
But he who hides his eyes will have many curses.
(Prov. 28:27)

He covets greedily all day long,
But the righteous gives and does not spare. (Prov. 21:26)

He who has pity on the poor lends to the LORD,
And He will pay back what he has given. (Prov. 19:17)

I have been young, and now am old, yet I have not seen
the righteous forsaken or their children begging bread.
They are ever giving liberally and lending, and their
children become a blessing. (Ps. 37:25–26 NRSV)

But when you do a charitable deed, do not let your left
hand know what your right hand is doing, that your
charitable deed may be in secret; and your Father who
sees in secret will Himself reward you openly.
(Matt. 6:3–4)

If you live right, the reward is a good life; if you are evil,
all you have is sin. (Prov. 10:16 CEV)

Sometimes you can become rich by being generous or
poor by being greedy.
Generosity will be rewarded:
Give a cup of water, and you will receive a cup of water
in return. (Prov. 11:24–25 CEV)

The Corporate Grapevine

Where there is no wood, the fire goes out;
And where there is no talebearer, strife ceases.
(Prov. 26:20)

If you have good sense, you will learn all you can,
but foolish talk will soon destroy you.
(Prov. 10:14 CEV)

Worthless people plan trouble.
Even their words burn like a flaming fire.
Gossip is no good!
It causes hard feelings and comes between friends.
(Prov. 16:27–28 CEV)

Did you hear of the diet plan hyped several years ago on ABC's "Good Morning America"? The anchorman interviewed Joey Skaggs about this new diet regimen that essentially involved a team of strongmen who followed the dieter around and physically restrained him from eating.

Well, if you're interested and would like to give Joey Skaggs a call, don't. He'll laugh in your face, just like he did all the others who phoned him from all over the world. Skaggs, a Greenwich Village media hoax artist, thinks it great fun to plant phony stories such as this new diet regimen and see how far the rumors spread. He is rarely disappointed, as the chagrined ABC officials learned when their interview story and subject were exposed.

The nuclear plant disaster at Chernobyl serves as still another example, a much more serious one, of rumor run rampant. Although the Soviet Union didn't allow first-hand reporting on the incident, reporters, pressed by their bosses for a story — *any* story — came up with vastly inflated casualty figures of about 2,000. A sister rumor was that Soviet Union plants lacked the safety features found in all U.S. plants. Several weeks later, both rumors turned out to be false, but the corrections got very little media coverage.

More recently, rumors about the Desert Storm operation surfaced everywhere. While I was at a client's office, an employee broke into our meeting with this announcement: "We just began bombing Iraq and the Iraqis have retaliated with chemicals. Our soldiers are falling everywhere from the poisonous gas." I learned the truth only hours later when, after our meeting broke up, I returned to my hotel room and watched CNN.

CNN also recently confessed their last-minute decision not to air an unconfirmed story about then-President Bush's collapse during his 1992 Far East trade negotiations trip. Their never-broadcast story claimed Bush was a victim of poisoning rather than the flu.

Winston Churchill once claimed, "A lie gets halfway around the world before the truth puts on its boots." To bring it closer to the office, let's put it this way: Gossip gets to the employee lounge before the facts come through the computer cable.

Why is the business office such a fertile ground for gossip about other people's lives and the company's problems? For some, it's idleness; they have nothing more constructive to occupy their time. For others, sharing "the latest" about little-known situations makes them feel important. For still others, giving inside information wins friends. Those who gossip for such reasons lack self-esteem and need to find more appropriate ways to build their confidence.

Gossip has been well defined as the practice of putting two and two together and making five. Sometimes, even *listening* to others' gossip is what makes it five. Be careful about responding to gossip with comments such as the following: "I can certainly see why you're upset" or "I don't blame you in the least" or "Well, I wondered why so-and-so didn't come into the meeting today; I guess that's why." Such responses are often assimilated into the gossiper's tale and you are then cited during the next recitation.

Even if the gossiper and the listener don't suffer any personal consequences from getting involved in somebody else's conflict, other unanticipated harm may result.

In the early 1980s, the Gulf Oil Chemical Company located in Baytown, Texas, was the victim of bomb threats and attempted extortion of $15 million. During the investigation by the company and FBI officials, rumors were rampant among workers about the contents of extortion letters mailed to Gulf:

- The money was to be parachuted from a company plane. The plant was selected because of its isolation.
- The extortionists warned that another plant — one closer to a residential area — would be a likely target for bombs if the demands were not met.
- The extortionists included three people or groups: someone who masterminded the plan, someone who built the devices, and someone who planted them. Corporate headquarters might also be a target.
- The extortionists told the Gulf officials that they would easily find the first five devices but would have difficulty with the last four.

Can you imagine the unrest, the activity, and the cost involved in containing those various rumors — none of which was true — until the FBI finished its investigation and the matter came under closer examination in the later court proceedings?

Even having the facts straight is no excuse for passing them on!

Almost every company has a similar story to tell. For years, a rumor has floated around that a portion of Procter and Gamble's profits is going to the church of Satan. This story, often spread in religious circles, has cost the company untold damage.

Even "harmless" gossip can produce sudden stress. After the first morning break in a seminar I was conducting for older employees at a client's site, attendees rumbled back into our meeting room quite alarmed. Rumor had just hit the twelfth floor that the company was about to be bought out. By late afternoon break, the hostile-take-over rumors had four different companies supposedly moving to buy out the client organization. Needless to say, the older employees, worried about their retirement options, got little out of the seminar topic that day. All rumors later proved to be false.

The next time you're tempted to share a story, ask yourself: Has this story been verified? Will anybody or any situation be helped by my passing on this information? Will any person, project, or relationship be jeopardized by my passing on this information? What is my motive for talking or listening? When in doubt, leave it out.

Gossip is expensive; it costs character as well as hard dollars. The English author Francis Quarles concludes: "Where lies are easily admitted, the father of lies will not easily be kept out."

For Further Reflection:

Stay away from gossips — they tell everything.
(Prov. 20:19 CEV)

A gossip tells everything, but a true friend will keep a secret. (Prov. 11:13 CEV)

The words of a talebearer are like tasty trifles,
And they go down into the inmost body. (Prov. 26:22)

Gratitude on This Gravy?

Give thanks in all circumstances; for this is the
will of God in Christ Jesus for you.
(1 Thess. 5:18 NRSV)

Keep your lives free from the love of money,
and be content with what you have; for he has said,
"I will never leave you or forsake you."
(Heb. 13:5 NRSV)

They call it take-home pay because there's no other
place you can afford to go with it.

Such quips are seemingly rather harmless, but some
people become embittered by such sentiments. They use
their paycheck as an excuse for lack of productivity on
the job and even as an excuse for stealing from their
employer.

Others, who would never think of actually stealing from
an employer, nevertheless, suffer from the "grass is always
greener-on-the-other-payroll" perspective. "And Joshua
said, 'Alas, Lord GOD, why have You brought this people
over the Jordan at all—to deliver us into the hand of the
Amorites, to destroy us? Oh, that we had been content, and
dwelt on the other side of the Jordan!'" (Josh. 7:7).

Haven't we all known persons who left low-paying
jobs for something else that they ultimately found

inconvenient, stressful, and unfulfilling? Sometimes the new tasks, demands, and trade-offs aren't as easy to cope with as we first imagined. In other words, the green grass on the other side of the fence has to be mowed, too.

Aside from the grass-is-always-greener philosophy, another reason we tend to feel discontent with our wages involves pride. The more prideful we are, the more we think we deserve. When asked how much they earn, employees often reply, "Twice what the boss thinks I'm worth and half what I deserve." It's very difficult for a proud individual to give an honest evaluation of what he or she contributes to the organization's efforts in reaching its goals.

The issues of self-esteem, self-confidence, and pride all raise their head during job interviews and performance-appraisal discussions. Recently, we interviewed applicants for a sales position. You might be surprised at the range of salary expectations and the reasoning behind those expectations:

- "I expect to start at $50,000" (from a college senior looking for her first job).
- "I don't want a base salary. I want all compensation to be on a commission basis. I know what I can do" (from a small-business owner who'd been in sales for thirteen years).
- "Fifteen to $18,000 would be appropriate. I've been out of work for a year and have a heart condition" (from a fifty-year-old with twenty years of applicable experience in our industry).

- "I'm looking for $30,000. I've had two years' experience in real estate. Although I haven't done particularly well there, that's because of the economy" (from a twenty-eight year old with two years' unrelated experience).

Pride often colors our expectations and our attitude of gratitude.

A focus on what we *lack* rather than on what we *have* is still another reason we feel discontent. There's an old story about the man who complained that he had no money to buy shoes until he met a man who had no feet.

We value such learning experiences about gratefulness for our children. A friend of mine told me about his teenage daughter's reaction to poverty while on a youth mission trip. She had stayed with a poor family in the community where they were conducting Bible schools, and upon her return to her affluent home and parents, she tried hard to describe the depth of the poverty she had seen. "Did you know those poor people didn't even have light switches on the wall?" In all her eighteen years, she had never seen a naked light bulb hanging by its cord from the ceiling!

Perspective is everything. Don't you imagine God looks upon our sheltered existence in much the same way these parents looked on their daughter's experience?

We may not be the best-paid employee in the city, but we are probably not the worst-paid either. Perseverance and gratefulness may play as much a part in our lives as talent and reward.

At the age of thirty-eight, Johann Sebastian Bach had to compete with five others for the job of choirmaster at St. Thomas Church, Leipzig. He got the job — not because of his already growing musical reputation, but because he alone agreed to teach Latin five days a week to elementary-age children in the church school!

Gratitude may also originate from contentment and opportunity rather than salary. At a client's office recently, I talked with a man in his early fifties about his job. For his age and years with the company, to me his job seemed rather routine and unchallenging. When I asked him how he liked his work, he responded: "It's the perfect job. The real benefit is that it's so routine I can do things without thinking. And that leaves me free to think about my art. I paint in the evenings and show my work on weekends. This job pays enough to get by and allows me time and energy for what I enjoy after hours."

Gratitude is not a matter of luck or talent or wealth. It's a mental attitude. Does your life seem to be one long, drawn-out sigh? If so, gratitude is the gravy that can make life's problems more palatable. Rather than a grumbling glare and a forward-looking prayer asking for more of God's blessings, perhaps we should glance backward and offer thanksgiving. Gratitude often becomes the root of many other virtues.

For Further Reflection:

Giving thanks always for all things to God the Father in the name of our Lord Jesus Christ. (Eph. 5:20)

Not that I am referring to being in need; for I have learned to be content with whatever I have. I know what it is to have little, and I know what it is to have plenty. In any and all circumstances I have learned the secret of being well-fed and of going hungry, of having plenty and of being in need. I can do all things through him who strengthens me. (Phil. 4:11–13 NRSV)

Greedy Piranhas

For the love of money is a root of all kinds of evil, for
which some have strayed from the faith in their greediness,
and pierced themselves through with many sorrows.
(1 Tim. 6:10)

Hell and Destruction are never full;
So the eyes of man are never satisfied.
(Prov. 27:20)

And He said to them, "Take heed and beware of
covetousness, for one's life does not consist in the
abundance of the things he possesses."
(Luke 12:15)

Y ou've heard it said that one can never be too rich or
too thin. I dare to differ — at least on the rich part.
You can be too rich when your jewelry spends more time
in the bank's safe than on your body. You can be too rich
when everything you own needs to be dry-cleaned. You
can be too rich when your parakeets have pedigree
papers. You can be too rich when your chauffeurs must
hire assistants. You can be too rich when your distant
relatives read the daily obituary columns in your city's
newspapers.

Most of us have a difficult time seriously drawing the
line between enough and not enough. Perhaps the line

forms around our *attitude* about money rather than the green stuff itself: Poverty will make you long for better food and clothes. Money will whet your appetite for luxuries. Greed will lead you to put the other person out of business.

Such are the attitudes often found on Wall Street among the likes of Dennis Levine and Ivan Boesky, who blazed quite a trail of greed followed by Michael Milken and innumerable executives at savings and loans institutions. In May 1986, Levine, of Drexel Burnham Lambert, was charged with raking in $12.6 million on insider-trading deals. When he agreed to cooperate, others got in the line of fire. Ivan Boesky agreed to pay a $100 million penalty for trading on inside information and also began to name others. The savings and loan list still goes on. And on.

What is the general public's attitude about such shenanigans? Well, if my daily phone calls are any indication, most people don't blink an eye. After the first Wall Street scandals broke several years ago, I continued to get calls from brokers asking for my trust, confiding that they "have done really well for some of their clients," and promising to do the same for me. In fact, one broker even laughed off the Boesky-Levine scandal, implying that, if anything, it had helped his business.

Our marketplace is full of such "get while the getting's good," "dog eat dog," and "get rich quick" attitudes and schemes. And they aren't all on Wall Street. They involve healthcare, higher education, and oil and gas. As a matter of fact, can you think of any industry free from such greed?

Corporations promote greed; individuals promote greed. Recently, my college-age son was duped into jeopardizing his college education by a group of people involved in a pyramid selling scheme. Why pursue a college degree, they said, when you could become rich almost overnight by selling our product? My son dropped out of school at mid-semester to sell the product. His enthusiasm lasted almost three months — until he learned the sales appointments were not made quite so easily as claimed, that the product didn't exactly "sell itself," that "instant success" could take a lifetime, that achievement couldn't necessarily be measured in a paycheck.

Another of the greed-for-the-common-man schemes played in hotel rooms around the country was a game called Airplane. The idea was to set up seats to resemble a passenger plane. The game participants talked colleagues into paying $1,000 for a seat and joining the game. As each new passenger joined the airplane, the others moved up toward the pilot's seat. The object of the scheme was to reach the pilot's quarters and bail out with the whole bundle of money. The risky part was keeping the game going long enough until you reached the front of the plane and got your loot. Most lost.

Not only does greed lead people into such illegal pastimes that show no regard for their fellowman, it even damages or destroys their own families. Children and spouses have been sacrificed to the philosophy of "just a little more." Enough would bring the working parent home at dinner time; greed brings him or her home much later. Enough means a five-day workweek; greed demands the weekend. In corporate America, we have many families molded around the office, rather than the job molded around the family.

Greed leads us to betray friendships. Many have sacrificed lifelong friendships over money disputes. Rather than give up their "right" to a few thousand dollars, people have ended relationships and sacrificed friends that would have provided great comfort and security through the years.

Others have betrayed friendships simply by neglect. When work competes for time with playing, eating, and talking together, friends often decide that making an extra dollar is of more lasting value than friendship. I hear people regretfully mourn the loss of time spent with friends they used to have, blaming it on the excessive demands of a job. Yet, who is holding the reigns of that runaway career?

Greed compromises morals. Jail terms handed out to numerous television evangelists underscore the cost of moral compromises. Paul warned about false teachers and preachers in his day, those who told people what they wanted to hear so they would be popular and well supported financially.

In our modern office, greed demands that we make our smaller competitors beg for a living, turn a deaf ear to employees asking for fair wages, spurn any requests from charities, cheat on our taxes, sell inferior and unsafe products, and accept kickbacks for bid approvals.

News stories of highly salaried corporate or political figures being indicted for accepting a kickback of only a few thousand dollars used to puzzle me. I was amazed that someone of wealth and position would risk so much for so little. But it finally dawned on me that logic is not at work in such matters; greed is. Only out-of-control greed (if there's any such thing as greed under control) could push logic, much less morality, out of the way. Why else would an executive earning $400,000 per year jeopardize that salary for the promise of an extra, illegal $3,000?

But greed leaves its most serious marks on our relationship to God. The only record we have of Jesus' anger was His condemnation of the money changers in the temple. Profit on the street was not enough for them; their love of money brought them right into the temple with their wares. The love of money reared its face at least three times at Jesus' death. Judas took his thirty pieces of silver, the soldiers cast lots for His garments at the cross, and soldiers at the graveside took their bribe to lie about His resurrection.

Men today are still controlled and compromised by their greed. The Bible has more to say about money than it has to say about either heaven or hell. Shouldn't we give greed closer scrutiny, even if our business isn't located on Wall Street?

For Further Reflection:

Yes, they are greedy dogs
Which never have enough.

And they are shepherds
Who cannot understand;
They all look to their own way,
Every one for his own gain,
From his own territory. (Isa. 56:11)

A faithful man will abound with blessings,
But he who hastens to be rich will not go unpunished. . . .
A man with an evil eye hastens after riches,
And does not consider that poverty will come upon him.
(Prov. 28:20, 22)

He covets greedily all day long,
But the righteous gives and does not spare. (Prov. 21:26)

He who is greedy for gain troubles his own house,
But he who hates bribes will live. (Prov. 15:27)

Some give freely, yet grow all the richer; others withhold
what is due, and only suffer want.
A generous person will be enriched, and one who gives
water will get water.
The people curse those who hold back grain, but a
blessing is on the head of those who sell it.
(Prov. 11:24–26 NRSV)

Staying Flexible When You Stand on Absolutes

When God blesses his people, their city prospers,
but deceitful liars can destroy a city.
(Prov. 11:11 CEV)

You are the light of the world. A city that is set on a hill
cannot be hidden. Nor do they light a lamp and put it under
a basket, but on a lampstand, and it gives light to all who are
in the house. Let your light so shine before men, that they
may see your good works and glorify your Father in heaven.
(Matt. 5:14–16)

"Influence is the exhalation of character," observes
Scottish clergyman W. M. Taylor. And Englishman
George Bulwer notes, "A good man does good merely
by living."

A restaurant owner in Irving, Texas, although he had
been through difficult days, refused to recognize any
need of God in his life. Because of his addiction to
alcohol, he'd lost his home, family, and business. Finally,
he was reduced to writing hot checks for his immediate
physical needs, and as a result was sentenced to several
months in prison. When he returned to our community
and was reunited with his family, the local pastor sent
church members to his door to share their faith. A

converted drug addict, a converted alcoholic, and a converted exconvict all made their way to him to try to say something that would influence him to accept God in his life and change his lifestyle. All to no avail.

Several years later, a young evangelist came to the church and shared his simple experience of growing up in a Christian home, of being converted at an early age, and preaching the Gospel since the age of twenty. The restaurant owner responded and committed his life to God.

The church community was puzzled. Why had he not identified with and responded to the others, who had led early lives similar to his own? What had this young evangelist said that got through to him? The restaurant owner responded, "I always figured all these other guys, the addicts, had just turned over a new leaf. I figured it was only a matter of time until they were back in the gutter. But this guy told me about a God that had kept him away from all that garbage for his entire life. A God big enough to do that got my attention."

Most of us will never know how far the influence of a godly life reaches. The admirable character that philosophers have referred to can express itself in many ways in the marketplace: by word, deed, or attitude.

I recently missed one of my chances. I was hurriedly scribbling at the flipchart in the conference room when a manager from the client organization stepped in through the doorway behind me with this greeting: "Welcome back, we haven't seen you around in a while. How have you been this last year? What's the oil glut doing to your business?"

I proceeded to answer her in detail with, I'm afraid, a discouraged, defeated look and tone. When I finished my monologue through the doldrums, she responded, "Isn't that always the way it goes? When things really get going well, it's almost like there's a God up there who decides to zap you off your feet for a good laugh."

Her bitter retort and chuckle so startled me that I couldn't reply. She wasn't a Christian, and to her way of thinking, my defeatist tale had just reinforced her erroneous view of God. How many times in the past had what I said or what I'd not said led people away from, and not toward God? The influence of idle words or unspoken words can't be underestimated.

On other occasions, I've been more alert to the opportunity to influence and shape another's philosophy and lifestyle. Recently, a colleague of mine was in the throes of a decision to leave her secure corporate salary and start her own business. At lunch, she asked me point-blank, "So many people don't make it; tell me, to what do you owe your success?" This time the opportunity to influence, to share my faith, hit me in the face.

But many people extend their realm of influence in the marketplace only to the negatives, the attitudes or activities of which they *don't* approve. That is, they're against office affairs, dishonesty in recordkeeping, wild partying, illegal wiretaps, Communism, lying, and profanity. That's all well and good.

But what are we Christians in the work force actually *for?* Are we initiating positive influences?

To paraphrase Galatians 5:17, are we showing love? Have we organized corporate tutoring programs for the disadvantaged? Are we writing company policies, devising campaigns, and soliciting donations for charity? Have we invited an unlovable colleague to lunch? Have we tried to restore a coworker's destroyed reputation?

Are we influencing with joy? Do we have a congenial spirit? Do we add energy to the office? Do we inspire hope when our colleagues feel defeated?

Are we sowing peace? Do we listen to gossip or squelch it? Do we pass on good comments one colleague has said about the other that might serve as a means of reconciliation? Do we actively try to resolve conflict, or simply choose to stay out of it?

Do we set an example of patience and gentleness? Are we the person others turn to if they have to ask for a repeat of instructions, or do others hide their mistakes from us, in fear of an angry, insulting outburst over the error? Do colleagues hate to be the ones to pass on bad news to us because of our harsh reactions? Do we encourage and provide for professional growth experiences for those we supervise?

Are we faithful? Can others count on us to keep the promises we make in meetings and on the telephone? Do we meet deadlines? Do we do quality work? Can others count on us to be the same to all people, showing no partiality? Can others count on our consistency in our moral choices?

Do we influence others by exemplifying self-control and moderation? Do we respect the body God has given us? Do we eat, rest, and exercise properly?

Even nature observes the effects of influence. As Pascal noted, "The least movement is of importance to all nature. The entire ocean is affected by a pebble." How much of your business environment do you affect for the better when you talk, act, and react within your company?

For Further Reflection:

Indeed, all who want to live a godly life in Christ Jesus will be persecuted. But wicked people and impostors will go from bad to worse, deceiving others and being deceived. But as for you, continue in what you have learned and firmly believed, knowing from whom you learned it, and how from childhood you have known the sacred writings that are able to instruct you for salvation through faith in Christ Jesus. (2 Tim. 3:12–15 NRSV)

My son, if sinners entice you,
Do not consent. (Prov. 1:10)

But you shall receive power when the Holy Spirit has come upon you; and you shall be witnesses to Me in Jerusalem, and in all Judaea and Samaria, and to the end of the earth. (Acts 1:8)

For though I am free from all men, I have made myself a servant to all, that I might win the more; and to the Jews I became as a Jew, that I might win Jews; to those who are under the law, as under the law, that I might win those who are under the law; to those who are without law, as without law (not being without law toward God, but under law toward Christ), that I might win those who are without law; to the weak I became as weak, that I might win the weak. I have become all things to all men, that I might by all means save some. (1 Cor. 9:19–22)

Teaching an Old Employee New Tricks

It's stupid and embarrassing to give an answer before you listen. . . . Everyone with good sense wants to learn.
(Prov. 18:13, 15 CEV)

Through wisdom a house is built
And by understanding it is established;
By knowledge the rooms are filled
With all precious and pleasant riches.
A wise man is strong,
Yes, a man of knowledge increases strength.
(Prov. 24:3–5)

Available information now doubles every twenty months, according to John Naisbitt, author of the best-seller *Megatrends 2000* and a periodic newsletter. Occasionally we hear those who extol ignorance and display false humility, as if they were virtues: "Now, jurors, I'm just an ignorant country lawyer, but I think . . ." Some use ignorance as a common denominator: "I couldn't care less how this machine works, but . . ."

Ignorance is never a virtue, and what you don't know can certainly hurt you.

In the last few years, we've heard the term *knowledge worker* bandied around a great deal. In fact, the knowledge worker—the employee who gathers, distributes, analyzes, and interprets information—is the fastest growing segment of the work population. But as you can see from the Scriptures cited above, the acquiring of knowledge has been important to individuals and society for a long time.

Only the emphasis has changed: The old philosopher advised, "Know thyself." The new philosopher advises, "Improve thyself." We as Americans spend $10-20 billion annually on personal growth seminars.

According to a report by the American Society for Training and Development, employers spend an estimated $210 billion a year to train their workers. But even with the current trend to rush to night classes on subjects ranging from toe painting to physics, some businesspeople are still reluctant.

Because I'm in the corporate training/education business myself, I often hear two opposing viewpoints about on-the-job learning: Some perceive it as a perk, and some see it as a punishment. Not infrequently in supervisory-skills courses, time-management courses, or sales courses, participants saunter into the classroom with a bored scowl and comment: "My boss sent me, I don't know why he's got it in for me, or what I did wrong." Usually, it doesn't take too long to figure out why the boss sent him! That attitude about learning usually explains a multitude of other problems on the job.

Learning is a lifelong effort for everyone. But to the wise businessperson, learning is a job perk. In fact, some companies recruit cream-of-the-crop employees by emphasizing their educational-development programs. IBM is one such company, devoting more dollars to training than any other U.S. organization outside the federal government.

Will Rogers observed that we are all ignorant — only on different subjects. There is no shame in ignorance on matters that we've not been exposed to. Disgrace follows only when we're made aware of our ignorance and refuse to snuff it out with knowledge.

One knowledge-hungry — and successful — administrative assistant crossed my path several years ago. In response to my question about her success and high salary as an administrative assistant, she explained that she had no formal higher education, but that she had made learning a lifelong habit, every day. She worked for three executive vice-presidents and after completing each project, if she didn't fully understand *why* as well as *what,* she made it a habit to follow up. "When you have a spare moment, I need a lesson," she would say. "I need to know why or how about X or Y." Flattered, her mentors shared their knowledge gladly. Her range of expertise still amazes me.

Among my own acquaintances, I've noticed that the higher up in the organization someone is, the more appreciative they seem to be of the opportunity to acquire new knowledge or skills.

When employees stop learning, they start a downward slide. When leaders quit learning about things around them and lose their sense of awareness about new trends, they become closed-minded. To survive, they must hire consultants or new employees to come into their organizations and give them newer, broader perspectives on problems.

As 1 Corinthians 8:1 warns, most often when we think we have all the answers, we'll soon find that we don't even know all the right questions! The more knowledge we gain, the more aware we become of how much knowledge there is to master. If you've ever sat across the conference table from a know-it-all, that very attitude confirms your creeping uneasiness that you probably need to check further for more information. When someone becomes totally closed to new ideas, we begin to see the limit of his or her knowledge.

Most of us have quoted Alexander Pope on occasion: "A little learning is a dangerous thing." We don't have to be nearly so cautious of the deceptive employee as we do of the honest worker who simply doesn't know what he's doing — and goes about it with fervor!

Along with the Bible's admonition about the virtue of acquiring knowledge, we also need to keep in mind certain precautions.

First, be cautious about any pride because of acquired knowledge. The old adage that there's always room to grow came to mind most recently when my assistant corrected me. With a master's degree in English and twelve years' experience in teaching writing courses to corporate clients under my belt, I thought I knew a thing or two about the English language. Recently, however, when I recorded an audio script segment, my assistant and the technical editor doubled into laughter at my pronunciation of the word *facade.* I'd written the word correctly in the script, but somehow, during my entire lifetime, I'd never connected the oral pronunciation to that written word. And I was reminded again how much I haven't yet learned in my own field — not to mention in the rest of the world.

Knowledge and humility go hand in hand. Treat knowledge like an automobile. When someone needs a ride, pull the car out of the garage and take them where they need to go. But there's no need to drive down to the bus stop every twenty minutes and honk your horn at the pedestrians waiting in the rain. Learning and humility complement each other.

A second precaution: Don't be duped by the simplicity of knowledge and wisdom. Some of the greatest truths are so simple we tend to downplay them or forget them until they slap us in the face again in the midst of difficulty. Consider: "Haste makes waste." "The love of money is the root of all evil." "A person is known by the company he keeps." "Pride goes before a fall." Don't let the simplicity of knowledge diminish its significance to you.

My husband always shows great respect and admiration for the talents of those who work with their hands. Although he has a master's degree in psychology and has been a knowledge worker all his life, he often admires the work of a carpenter or a gardener. *Significant* work is *any* work that makes the world a better place and fulfills a human need.

A final precaution about knowledge: Be careful to gain knowledge of the right things. Psalm 111:10 tells us the fear of the Lord is the beginning of wisdom. And as the Apostle Paul admonishes in 2 Timothy 2:15, we gain that fear and knowledge of the Lord through Bible study and contemplation of the truths exposed there.

It has been said that knowledge is power; and knowledge of the ways of the Lord allows us access to both the world's knowledge and God's power.

For Further Reflection:

Buy truth, and do not sell it; buy wisdom, instruction, and understanding. (Prov. 23:23 NRSV)

An intelligent mind acquires knowledge, and the ear of the wise seeks knowledge. (Prov. 18:15 NRSV)

Take my instruction instead of silver, and knowledge rather than choice gold. (Prov. 8:10 NRSV)

The wise lay up knowledge, but the babbling of a fool brings ruin near. (Prov. 10:14 NRSV)

Why should fools have money for an education when they refuse to learn? (Prov. 17:16 CEV)

Teach me good judgment and knowledge, for I believe in your commandments. (Ps. 119:66 NRSV)

For the protection of wisdom is like the protection of money, and the advantage of knowledge is that wisdom gives life to the one who possesses it. (Eccl. 7:12 NRSV)

Listening and Other Lowly Habits

You will say the wrong thing if you talk too much — so be
sensible and watch what you say.
The words of a good person are like pure silver, but the
thoughts of an evil person are almost worthless.
(Prov. 10:19–20 CEV)

Some who have nothing may pretend to be rich, and some
who have everything may pretend to be poor.
(Prov. 13:7 CEV)

Several years ago, M. David Lowe Personnel Agency surveyed 200 Houston workers to ask for their suggested New Year's resolutions for their bosses. The most frequently mentioned resolution was "Communicate more with staff." The employees got even more specific on various aspects of communication when they gave other suggestions: Learn to listen, be more open to staff suggestions, give more praise, learn more about what your employees do, learn your employees' names. Most of their answers had to do with listening, not talking.

Although we often think of communication as a fifty-fifty proposition, we're usually splitting the percentage between people: 50 percent effort on one person's part and 50 percent effort on the other person's part. But consider that percentage solely in your own communication patterns: 50 percent talking and 50 percent listening. It takes skill in both areas to be adequate on the job.

Perhaps we don't hear God when He speaks to us because we don't get much practice in listening to other people. Jesus knew when to talk and when to listen. Coming into the district of Caesarea Philippi, He asked His disciples, "Who do men say that I, the Son of Man, am?" (Matt. 16:13).

You'll notice that Jesus didn't begin by lecturing on His identity. Instead, He asked a question. What had they observed and absorbed by being with Him during His ministry? What opinion did the crowds have of Him? In other words, He was getting feedback, checking His perception of their understanding.

With the Samaritan woman at the well, He used a different technique. He communicated His identity to her by telling her that He was the Living Water and the possessor of eternal life (John 4).

The writer of Ecclesiastes tells us that there's a time for both sides of communication, a time to speak and a time to keep silent. But I have a hunch that most of us spend far too much time talking and not enough time listening. Do you recognize any of the following attitudes in your own listening habits?

I-don't-understand. (You don't pay attention because you think the subject is too complex. What's more, you're not interested enough to put forth the effort to learn.)

I-know-what-you-mean. (You assume you know what the talker thinks or feels and don't bother to check to see if your perception is correct.)

I've-got-my-mind-made-up. (You've already made up your mind about the issue, no matter what the other person says. During the talker's effort to express an opinion, you're concentrating on how you'll present your own views when he or she is finished. In fact, the few details you do catch, you plan to use as ammunition in your rebuttal.)

That's-off-the-wall. (You make a snap judgment, refusing to consider unusual ideas, plans, opinions, or feelings.)

I-don't-want-to-get-involved. (You mean, "Don't tell me your problems. I've got my own." We often divert the talker with, "Speaking of reports being due, that reminds me, I need . . .")

Hmmmm . . . (I-don't-like-you). (You don't like the way someone dresses, walks, or sells shoes, so you're closed to anything the person has to say on any subject.)

Listening is not only beneficial to the person doing the talking; good listening habits are to our own advantage. The English dramatist and novelist Oliver Goldsmith observed: "Every absurdity has a champion to defend it, for error is always talkative." Perhaps an easy way to reduce our own error factor on the job is to talk less and listen more.

At a recent five-day workshop, the person who introduced me to the audience mentioned that I'd written twelve books in the area of corporate communication. Then she held up copies of some of those books. Then for five days, we used two of the books as course texts, referring to them at least two or three times a day. At the end of the week, an attendee stopped to shake hands with me and tell me how much he'd enjoyed the course. In all seriousness he asked, "Have you ever thought of writing a book on this subject?"

In the next business meeting that you conduct or attend, observe those around you and see if you don't agree with the following observations:

> Be always less willing to speak than to hear; what thou hearest, thou receivest; what thou speakest thou givest. — It is more glorious to give, but more profitable to receive.
> —Francis Quarles, English author

> It is the characteristic of great wits to say much in few words, so it is of small wits to talk much and say nothing.
> —La Rochefoucauld, French courtier

People who consider themselves great communicators often talk just because they can express themselves well, rather than because their ideas are sound and profitable.

If Jesus felt the need to ask questions and listen to His friends for feedback, how much more should we check our perceptions and improve ourselves by listening?

Here's how:

- Be aware of your own bad listening habits and attitudes.
- Be silent occasionally to give others a chance to speak.
- Open the door for others with phrases like, "What do you think about . . . ?"
- Focus your whole body on the listening; "be there" without shuffling papers or jiggling your keys while others speak.
- Ask questions when you don't understand.
- Ask questions to check that you really understood.
- Listen between the lines, to the feelings as well as the words.
- Express understanding.
- Summarize to yourself what the other person said and decide if you need to do something, change something, or improve something about yourself and the way you do business.

By listening, we learn what might not come to our attention any other way.

For Further Reflection:

My child, listen carefully to everything I say.
(Prov. 4:20 CEV)

Even a fool is counted wise when he holds his peace;
When he shuts his lips, he is considered perceptive.
(Prov. 17:28)

An ignorant fool learns by seeing others punished;
a sensible person learns by being instructed.
(Prov. 21:11 CEV)

My son, pay attention to my wisdom;
Lend your ear to my understanding,
That you may preserve discretion,
And your lips may keep knowledge. (Prov. 5:1–2)

I will hear what God the LORD will speak,
For He will speak peace
To His people and to His saints;
But let them not turn back to folly. (Ps. 85:8)

Just Sign on the Dotted Line ...

My child, suppose you agree to pay the debt of someone,
who cannot repay a loan.
Then you are trapped by your own words, and you are
now in the power of someone else.
Here is what you should do:
Go and beg for permission to call off the agreement.
Do this before you fall asleep or even get sleepy.
Save yourself, just as a deer or a bird tries
to escape from a hunter.
(Prov. 6:1–5 CEV)

It's a dangerous thing to guarantee payment
for someone's debts.
Don't do it!
(Prov. 11:15 CEV)

It's stupid to guarantee someone else's loan.
(Prov. 17:18 CEV)

"Creditors have better memories than debtors; they are a superstitious sect, great observers of set days and times," Ben Franklin wryly noted. If you've ever lent money to an acquaintance, you'll note how lenders not only become clock-watchers and calendar watchers, but also become behavior and attitude observers.

We see one of our debtors out eating pizza with his family on Tuesday night and wonder how he can afford it, owing us what he does. We phone his house, finding him still in bed in the morning, and pointedly remind him that we've been at work for hours.

We all have our differing interpretations when drawing the line between wants and needs — especially when others are using our money. I first became aware of the difference between my own and my college-age daughter's interpretation of necessities during her first year away at college. The first semester we did our best at estimating the costs of apartment living; we told her to keep track of her expenses, and we'd reevaluate her living allowance in about three months. At the end of that trial period, she concluded her allowance just wasn't enough.

When we sat down to discuss the issue, she presented her case. Strongly, I might add — until she let slip a comment about having a $15 manicure. After that, let's just say she had a hard time convincing us she needed more money to make ends meet.

The reverse also proves true. The borrower's attitude begins to change with regard to his benefactor's generosity. English essayist Joseph Addison defines a moneylender with that guarded perspective: "He serves you in the present tense; he lends you in the conditional mood; keeps you in the subjunctive; and ruins you in the future!" Consider the movie version of the stereotypical

Mr. Moneybags, who preys on the innocent by charging outrageous interest and calling in loans at the most inopportune times.

Through the years, an acquaintance of mine has created a situation whereby her nephew and his wife call to borrow money periodically. At first, the aunt met their every need. Then, when she took on more and more personal responsibilities, she was not financially able or inclined to help them every time they called. Now, rather than being grateful for past help, this couple feels the aunt has grown "selfish."

Whether you're the borrower or the lender, a loan changes forever the way each party sees the other. If you try to force the other person to pay, he or she becomes a sure enemy. If you don't ask for repayment, you may lose money you can't afford to forego and become bitter.

Friendship most often falls by the wayside.

Another reason to give yourself pause before lending money to an acquaintance is the consideration that you may not be really helping the other person when you help him or her go into debt. That individual may continue to do business or live beyond his or her means. When the person falls into debt up to the eyeballs and begins to feel waves of financial pressure, he may not think of you as a lifeguard with a raft but as a big gust of wind, blowing him farther from shore.

And while endorsing character can be embarrassing and unfruitful, endorsing another's credit can be downright expensive. In his younger days, my father agreed to a business partnership with the pastor of our small rural church. The minister had always been good with his hands in all kinds of electrical repair work; therefore, my father signed a note and agreed to put up the first $500 to open the shop where the pastor would ply his part-time trade repairing TVs and radios. A few weeks later, the pastor left town with the money — before the store opened its doors.

Nothing tests character — the borrower's or the lender's — like one's handling of credit.

So what should you do when asked to lend money? If you can afford to do so, give it. Generosity is Godlike.

For Further Reflection:

> Don't guarantee to pay someone else's debt.
> If you don't have the money, you might lose your bed.
> (Prov. 22:26–27 CEV)

> The world's poorest credit risk is the man who agrees to pay a stranger's debts. (Prov. 27:13 TLB)

Participative Management and Micaiah

Without counsel, plans go wrong, but
with many advisers they succeed.
(Prov. 15:22 NRSV)

Too much pride causes trouble.
Be sensible and take advice.
(Prov. 13:10 CEV)

We hear a lot today about Theory X and Theory Y managers. Theory X managers believe that employees are basically lazy and unmotivated, that they work solely for a paycheck as a reward, and that they have few creative ideas to contribute to the workplace. These managers conclude that such employees need authoritarian control and discipline.

Theory Y managers, on the other hand, believe that most workers are self-motivated, enjoy being productive, work for rewards other than a paycheck, and can contribute ideas on how to do their jobs better. They control themselves fairly well and work responsibly when given appropriate guidelines. These employees, Theory Y managers believe, need opportunities to grow and to participate in their own growth and that of their company.

Neither Theory X managers nor Theory Y managers are immune to mistakes. Authoritarian managers who listen to no one obviously ignore the Bible's admonition about the safety and assurance in seeking many opinions before making decisions.

But Theory Y managers can make the equally egregious mistake of listening to the wrong people at the wrong times. In effect, they clue others to what they want them to say, and they don't even bother to ask those employees who might give contradictory opinions. In staff meetings, they're the kind who ask with a scowl, "Does anybody have any *serious* objections to proceeding as I've outlined?" Total Quality Management (TQM) out the window.

Such was the case with King Ahab and the prophet Micaiah (2 Chron. 18). For three years, Syria and Israel had not gone to war. But during Judean King Jehoshaphat's visit to King Ahab of Israel, King Ahab began to grumble to his court officials about something not being right in the kingdom. Syria still occupied Ramoth Gilead, one of their cities. He asked his ally King Jehoshaphat if he were willing to join him in the effort to reclaim the city. King Jehoshaphat agreed, with the caution that they'd better ask the Lord first about the outcome.

When King Ahab asked his four hundred false prophets about the decision, they said, in effect, "Go for it. God'll give you a sure victory."

But King Jehoshaphat wasn't satisfied, "Aren't we leaving out somebody? Isn't there somebody else we should ask?"

Reluctantly, King Ahab called in Micaiah. When he was first asked, Micaiah agreed with the other prophets that King Ahab would be successful in battle just as the messenger sent to get him had advised him.

But we'll at least have to give the king credit for realizing when his man was giving advice under pressure. He gave him "permission" to say what he was really thinking and got the opposite advice: The word from the Lord was *not* to go to battle.

Do you think King Ahab was glad to be warned of his impending death? No. He had Micaiah thrown in prison to survive on bread and water until he, the king, returned victorious. Wishful thinking. Despite all his precautions to thwart the prophet's warning, King Ahab died in battle.

Several business truths shout from this story: First, as the proverb says, seek advisers.

And where are those advisers who perhaps can give insight into our decisions? Often right under our noses.

National surveys tell us that top managers made a big mistake in the 1980s. To keep good employees, they focused on the growth industries' allure of glittering compensation packages. These compensation packages contained unique perks unheard of in previous decades.

The ironic, surprising findings of more recent studies tell us that rather than big salaries and stock options, employees are more concerned about how management treats them. Career women and men insist that the work climate, standards for performance, and the work itself are what really make them feel good about their jobs. In other words, they like being allowed to participate in management decisions and challenging work.

But besides the value of allowing employees to be advisers on the job, bosses have to be careful about surrounding themselves with yes-men and women suffering from "group think." That is, they need to be careful not to foster an atmosphere where everybody feels pressure to fit into the mold and where the least risky common denominator among a group dictates the course of action.

One of the most valuable resources in my own job revolves around the opportunity to get advice and feedback from my husband, who works with me in the business. Although always supportive once our team makes a decision, we often play devil's advocate with each other to flesh out half-baked ideas. Many employee-employer relationships break down when it comes to seeking contrary advice. Just how far do you go in expressing opposition to an idea? Only deep security in a relationship produces that strength from both parties. Supervisors have to work at building that security, where employees know they're welcome to speak up honestly.

The overwhelming evidence is that businesspeople do care about the climate of their workplace, do want to be seen as individuals and challenged to take part in decisionmaking, and do care about the results. Our job, whether we are bosses or subordinates, is to ask for ideas from our coworkers and then evaluate those ideas fairly.

"Good intelligence is nine tenths of any battle," Napoleon insisted. Businesspeople who don't recognize the contribution of their coworkers to their own success and the organization's goals are dangerous people to have on the job.

For Further Reflection:

> Be sure you have sound advice before making plans or starting a war. (Prov. 20:18 CEV)

Sure Job Had Patience, but He Never Worked *Here*

> But those who wait on the LORD
> Shall renew their strength;
> They shall mount up with wings like eagles,
> They shall run and not be weary,
> They shall walk and not faint.
> (Isa. 40:31)

> My friends, be glad, even if you have a lot of trouble.
> You know that you learn to endure by having your faith
> tested. But you must learn to endure everything, so that
> you will be completely mature and not lacking in anything.
> (James 1:2–4 CEV)

> With patience a ruler may be persuaded,
> and a soft tongue can break bones.
> (Prov. 25:15 NRSV)

"There is as much difference between genuine patience and sullen endurance, as between the smile of love and the malicious gnashing of the teeth," insisted W. S. Plumer, nineteenth-century clergyman. While we wait and work, patience does *not* mean that we have to feel careless, cold-hearted, and condemned to non-productivity or failure.

Neither is patience a state of indifference, when we don't care about an outcome and consequently feel no urgency for change or action.

Actually, patience is a positive state, an *action* rather than a reaction. "The two powers which in my opinion constitute a wise man are those of bearing and forbearing," claimed Epictetus, the Roman philosopher. Bearing is choosing to work under pressure; forbearing is a conscious decision to extend patience to others, to accomplish objectives with whatever they offer or fail to offer.

Patience can often be power. With patience and power, the caterpillar becomes a moth. The patience of the negotiator in making his proposal builds a winning strategy. In fact, nothing marks an amateur so much as impatience in any kind of business effort — negotiations in particular. The Bible warns us not to rush into different business endeavors without preparing and counting the costs: "A wise man is cautious and avoids danger; a fool plunges ahead with great confidence" (Prov. 14:16 TLB).

Patience provides us with choices. After taking the dive, it's difficult to switch directions in midair. Hiring situations provide a real challenge in patience for most of us. Once we decide the workload warrants another staff member, we want them *now*. And the tendency is to hire the first qualified applicant that we interview. Big mistake.

Patience also improves our logic. We hear people in a pressure situation say, "I can't think on my feet," or, more aptly said, "I can't think under heat." In a rush situation, we often make strategic business errors, failing to see pitfalls along the path and even hurting people and relationships along the way to disaster. Patience allows time, circumstances, and other advisers to take off our blinders.

Patience improves our health. Physicians report that disorders such as asthma, allergies, ulcers, and heart disease are all stress related. Patience promotes control of our own lives and attitudes, thereby our blood pressure and energy level. We have all heard about Type-A personalities and the kinds of stress these people create for themselves and others. Signs of impatience are all around us. Impatient people

- Walk up escalators
- Jab at close-door buttons on elevators
- Harrumph and curse in the supermarket line
- Ask questions without waiting for answers
- Glare at their watches without noting the time

If you see yourself in any of the above, audit yourself more carefully. Identify what it is that stresses you, and then either eliminate that from your life or learn to deal with it. Accept the fact that stress is personal. To one person, a particular job is highly stressful; to another, the same job is low stress. How you react to the job creates or eliminates your stress.

Stress-management experts have devised several exercises to improve our patience level as well as our physical health. When you go into a restaurant with friends, force yourself to be the last person to finish eating. Or in freeway traffic, force yourself to drive at the speed limit in the right-hand lane. Again, remember patience is an action and a reaction.

Patience increases awareness. We begin to notice people around us, rather than being so involved in getting on with our own lives. We think of things to say to them and become aware of the time and attention we could lavish on them. In so doing, we make a difference in others' lives and enrich our own.

On a recent trip when I checked into the hotel, I was delayed at the registration desk while waiting for the bell captain to unload my luggage from the van. Rather than shuffle around irritated at the delay, my usual disposition when I've been traveling long hours, I became mesmerized by the young woman at the check-in desk. At such a late hour, she sounded so cheery on the phone and to people passing in the lobby. The first thing I'd noticed about her was that she was considerably overweight. But as I stood listening to her, her face took on a special countenance to match the lilt in her voice. The more I watched and listened to her check others in, the more my first impression of her changed to one of admiration for her genuine helpfulness to the guests. When the last guest left the counter, I said to her, "Pardon me for staring at you, but you have such a beautiful complexion." She broke into an even bigger smile. "Why, . . . thank you."

I could tell that the compliment pleased her as I walked away. The next day when I stopped at the desk to pick up my mail, she said, "You know, your compliment last night made my week."

Such a small thing. But to one who had probably focused on her weight for most of her life, the compliment took on added significance. The words cost so little effort. Patience provides opportunity to really look at those around us and make a difference in their lives, however small.

Patience makes us more tolerant of *ourselves*. We can't become more patient of other people without some of that patience spilling back onto us. We permit ourselves not to always be the first one through with a project, not to always arrive first at staff meetings. We forgive ourselves when we make "stupid" mistakes.

Finally, patience deepens our trust in God. According to the world, seeing is believing. According to God, believing is seeing. We learn that God's delays are not necessarily denials; we learn to give Him time to act on our behalf.

Many times God must see us the way we see TV sitcoms. We see the hero and the heroine, longing for each other's phone call, continue to miss each other. The heroine calls, and the hero is in the shower; by the time he gets to the phone, the ringing phone has stopped. We viewers feel that misconnection. Often because of our impatience in waiting for God's properly timed answers, we give up on Him and take the wrong action ourselves.

Although patience may be hard to define, we know the attitude or action when we see it:

- Patience indulges the meeting clown.
- Patience courteously asks for corrections.

- Patience avoids sulking while waiting for a return call.
- Patience tolerates the learning curve for others.
- Patience investigates before investing.
- Patience permits others to smile when you yourself cry.
- Patience prays rather than pouts.

As Swiss theologian Johann Lavater reminds us: "He surely is most in need of another's patience, who has none of his own."

For Further Reflection:

For you have need of endurance, so that after you have done the will of God, you may receive the promise. (Heb. 10:36)

Add to your faith virtue, to virtue knowledge, to knowledge self-control, to self-control perseverance, to perseverance godliness, to godliness brotherly kindness, and to brotherly kindness love. (2 Peter 1:5–7)

Now we exhort you, brethren, warn those who are unruly, comfort the fainthearted, uphold the weak, be patient with all. (1 Thess. 5:14)

God is the one who makes us patient and cheerful. I pray that he will help you live at peace with each other, as you follow Christ. (Rom. 15:5 CEV)

But you, O man of God, flee these things and pursue righteousness, godliness, faith, love, patience, gentleness. (1 Tim. 6:11)

And not only that, but we also glory in tribulations, knowing that tribulation produces perseverance; and perseverance, character; and character, hope. Now hope does not disappoint, because the love of God has been poured out in our hearts by the Holy Spirit who was given to us. (Rom. 5:3–5)

For examples of patience in suffering, look at the Lord's prophets. We know how happy they are now because they stayed true to him then, even though they suffered greatly for it. Job is an example of a man who continued to trust the Lord in sorrow; from his experiences we can see how the Lord's plan finally ended in good, for he is full of tenderness and mercy. (James 5:10 TLB)

Building Bigger Barns

We make our own plans, but the LORD decides
where we will go.
(Prov. 16:9 CEV)

When you see trouble coming, don't be stupid
and walk right into it — be smart and hide.
(Prov. 22:3 CEV)

Use wisdom and understanding to establish your home;
let good sense fill the rooms with priceless treasures.
(Prov. 24:3–4 CEV)

We humans make plans, but the LORD has the final word.
(Prov. 16:1 CEV)

You should know better than to say, "Today or tomorrow
we'll go to the city. We'll do business there for a year
and make a lot of money!" What do you know about
tomorrow? How can you be so sure about your life?
It is nothing more than mist that appears for only a little
while before it disappears. You should say, "If the Lord
lets us live, we will do these things." Yet you are
stupid enough to brag, and it is wrong to be so proud.
(James 4:13–16 CEV)

W̲ho could have known that the oil crisis of the 1970s
would turn into an oil glut a mere fifteen years

later? Who could have predicted the breakup of AT&T and the influx of multitudes of long-distance services? Before we heard the earth rumble, who could have forecast the earthquakes in Mexico City, Ecuador, Russia, California, and Turkey? Who would have hoped that we could fight a war in the Persian Gulf with as few as seventy-nine casualties? Who could have predicted the dismantling of the Berlin Wall or the dissolution of the Soviet Union?

Few would argue that we will always have unexpected political, financial, and natural upheavals in the world. But does that mean we as businesspeople should not plan for our future? That we should not make plans to open a branch office tomorrow? That we should not fund research on a cure for cancer? That we should not further our personal education or expand our experience to acquire a better future?

Just what is the relationship between the scriptures that tell us to plan for the future and those that caution against spending our money before we make it and presuming upon the length of our days?

According to the Small Business Administration, the majority of all new businesses fail within the first five years. That is not to say that a particular business idea was weak, but simply that people who immediately grab an idea and run with it often fail to match their product or service to the right market, or even to their own personal goals and qualifications for the job. Additionally, they find they're without adequate staff or financing.

Planning is no small matter.

Likewise with the large corporation. We have back-orders on Christmas toys. We build factories for manufacturing a new hoola-hoop, and then see them sit idle when the trend passes as quickly as it started. We see advertising for products that are never produced. We must return recalled autos to the dealer because someone didn't take the time to make all the proper safety tests. Signs of poor planning stand everywhere.

Yet few would disagree that planning is a must; it forces us to devote regular, directed time to the future. We must ask ourselves what valuable information or experience we should glean from any situation for application in the future. How should the current events change the way we think about our product or service? What opportunities do these events or circumstances offer for the way we do business? Planning makes tasks easier, reduces confusion, saves time, and gives everyone direction.

Yes, planning makes good business sense. And often the best planning is simply doing the present tasks well, with an eye toward duty and detail.

But to posture ourselves between planning and presumption, we should consider the proper attitude about both. Augustine said it best: "God will not suffer man to have a knowledge of things to come; for if he had prescience of his prosperity, he would be careless; and if understanding of his adversity, he would be despairing and senseless."

Too much focus on a dark future creates worry. During the 1991–1992 recession, those experiencing doom in their industry began to spread the despair to those in other jobs and fields. In a booming year in which we added staff and grew at an unprecedented rate, our anxiety grew as we listened to reports from those all around us about pending disaster. It was as if we had a tarp spread over our heads. Our balance sheet told us we were out of the rain, but we were afraid to let go the cover and dance in the sunlight.

In our case, worry of what *might* come dampened the joy that usually goes with growth.

When we worry, we fail to live today to its advantage and find little satisfaction in the small victories because we have a sense of impending doom. In the face of prosperity and success, we stand with stooped shoulders, as if braced for a falling timber across our backs.

On the other hand, presuming on a promising and prosperous future makes us self-reliant rather than God-reliant. We act carelessly toward our fellowman and disregard our duties to make the world a better place. What was once faith in God's providence becomes confidence in our own reasoning and expertise. We begin to think that our engineering ingenuity created the winning design. That our clever negotiating won the contract. That our communication skills got us the job.

And with that confidence comes pride and selfishness — the very opposites of Christlikeness in our lives.

Benjamin Franklin offered these observations about the part God's will plays in our planning: "The longer I live, the more convincing proofs I see of this truth, that God governs in the affairs of man; and if a sparrow cannot fall to the ground without His notice, is it probable that an empire can rise without His aid?"

Trust, yes. Be anxious, no. Plan, yes. Presume, no.

For Further Reflection:

If you have good sense, you will act sensibly, but fools act like fools. (Prov. 13:16 CEV)

For which of you, intending to build a tower, does not sit down first and count the cost, whether he has enough to finish it — lest, after he has laid the foundation, and is not able to finish, all who see it begin to mock him, saying, "This man began to build and was not able to finish." (Luke 14:28–30)

The plans of the diligent lead surely to abundance, but everyone who is hasty comes only to want. (Prov. 21:5 NRSV)

Be sensible and store up precious treasures — don't waste them like a fool. (Prov. 21:20 CEV)

You should take good care of your sheep and goats, because wealth and honor don't last forever.
After the hay is cut and the new growth appears and the harvest is over, you can sell lambs and goats to buy clothes and land.
From the milk of the goats, you can make enough cheese to feed your family and all your servants.
(Prov. 27:23-27 CEV)

The human mind may devise many plans, but it is the purpose of the LORD that will be established. (Prov. 19:21 NRSV)

Even if your army has horses ready for battle, the LORD will always win. (Prov. 21:31 CEV)

Do not boast about tomorrow,
For you do not know what a day may bring forth.
(Prov. 27:1)

James, John, and Power Politics

Our LORD and our God, victory doesn't come from
the east or the west or from the desert.
You are the one who judges.
You can take away power and give it to others.
(Ps. 75:6–7 CEV)

Did your parents ever leave the house for an evening
or for a few days and put an older brother or sister
in charge of you during their absence? Were you angry
or pleased at the new authority?

Have you ever thought about why the quest for authority and power by the Apostles James and John made
the other disciples angry (Mark 10:35–45)? Whether
James and John got to be hotshots really had little to do
with the other ten. Or did it?

What is it about another's power that disturbs us on
the job?

Power magnifies one's true character. Authority often
brings out the littleness in people. Plutarch observed:
"There is no stronger test of a man's real character than
power and authority, exciting as they do every passion,
and discovering every latent vice."

Many of us have made such an observation around the office. We know of bosses who, at the beginning of each year, whip out their calendars to record their vacations first and announce to everybody else that they should work around those times, regardless: regardless of another's child's graduation, an ill mother's planned birthday visit, or a long-planned trip with a spouse. We see managers whose greed leads them to make short-term profits at the expense of long-term benefits for the stockholders. We hear bosses pull rank to settle conflicts rather than get to the bottom of an issue.

But just as power brings out the pettiness or vice in some; it brings out the best in others. Abraham could have chosen the most fertile fields for his stock and sent Lot packing; however, he allowed his nephew first choice and took the leftover land for himself. Few in the business world follow his example when given the power to do otherwise.

The disciples may have become angry over James and John's request out of fear of the character traits that would rise to the surface with those two in charge.

Or, perhaps the other ten's attitude turned on simple jealousy.

You'll notice that when Jesus asked the two disciples if they were able to handle the responsibility that went with the power they sought, they answered with great confidence, "We are able." Many times we look with envy at those in positions of power and feel equally capable. But perhaps we'd do well to take a closer look at what power entails.

Power can be pain. Power can mean having to choose between two bad alternatives. A friend of mine recently had some difficult years, financially, resulting in his family having to sell their house and move into a less expensive one. With tears in his eyes, he told of a bigger regret: He had just had to terminate the employment of a dear friend who had worked for him for seventeen years.

Those in a position of power do not always face such grave consequences; nevertheless, few decisions are easy.

A friend of mine who manages an office of eighteen people lamented to me that she hadn't been able to get to the dentist with her painful tooth. When I asked her why she hadn't taken off work early on Friday afternoon, she explained her choices. Two other employees had already scheduled the day for vacation. Another had to go to school to meet with a child's teacher. Another felt as though she were coming down with the flu. Another got a call from the school, asking her to pick up a sick child. Another had asked to leave early to catch a flight out of town to join a spouse at a business conference. With company policy saying that no more than three could be away at once, she had a hard choice about whose claim was more urgent or "fair." And, of course, she canceled her own dentist appointment.

Power derived from a position of authority is not without its problems. Yet, some still strive for that magic wand of authority. James and John hoped to gain such power by their position as Jesus' right-hand men. Power still comes to many people through their position in the corporate hierarchy, and that power is theirs to use for the benefit of all concerned or to demean others and magnify their own pettiness.

But don't confuse such positional power with personal power. Although we don't all have our chance at the positional power bestowed by a corporate title, we all can have personal power.

Business management consultants and career experts often admonish fast trackers who want to get things done to forget the published chain of command and learn who has the real power. That real power has usually surfaced because of a person's moral character, ability to achieve results, and attachment to a good or great purpose.

Although authority possessed by virtue of one's paycheck, title, or influential parents or friends can't be pushed aside, the most powerfully effective people possess personal power; that is, they have energy, insight, and ideas. With their confidence and zeal, they inspire others to dream, to pursue excellence, and to sacrifice for the common good and a greater purpose. Having inspired, they communicate clear directives through personal example.

Always seek to develop personal power rather than positional power. That's the real measure of power and influence. Strive to be a leader that people would follow if given a *choice*.

For Further Reflection:

James and John, the sons of Zebedee, came forward to him and said to him, "Teacher, we want you to do for us whatever we ask of you." And he said to them, "What is it you want me to do for you?" And they said to him, "Grant us to sit, one at your right hand and one at your left, in your glory." But Jesus said to them, "You do not know what you are asking. Are you able to drink the cup that I drink, or be baptized with the baptism that I am baptized with?" They replied, "We are able." Then Jesus said to them, "The cup that I drink you will drink; and with the baptism with which I am baptized, you will be baptized; but to sit at my right hand or at my left is not mine to grant, but it is for those for whom it has been prepared." When the ten heard this, they began to be angry with James and John. So Jesus called them and said to them, "You know that among the Gentiles those whom they recognize as their rulers lord it over them, and their great ones are tyrants over them. But it is not so among you; but whoever wishes to become great among you must be your servant, and whoever wishes to be first among you must be slave of all. For the Son of Man came not to be served but to serve, and to give his life a ransom for many." (Mark 10:35–45 NRSV)

Pride: Did I Ever Tell You About the Time . . . ?

What is so special about you? What do you have
that you were not given? And if it was given to you,
how can you brag?
(1 Cor. 4:7 CEV)

I will break the pride of your power; I will make
your heavens like iron and your earth like bronze.
(Lev. 26:19)

A man's pride will bring him low,
But the humble in spirit will retain honor.
(Prov. 29:23)

For I say, through the grace given to me,
to everyone who is among you, not to think of himself
more highly than he ought to think, but to think soberly,
as God has dealt to each one a measure of faith.
(Rom. 12:3)

There is more hope for a fool than for someone who says,
"I'm really smart!"
(Prov. 26:12 CEV)

By humility and the fear of the LORD
Are riches and honor and life.
(Prov. 22:4)

Take your pulse on pride:

- Do you enjoy controlling access to people or information?
- Do you take pride in being able to give orders to others?
- Do you enjoy approving or rejecting others' plans?
- Do you keep a mental checklist of how your job skills rate in comparison to others?
- At performance appraisal time, do you wish you knew how everyone else was rated in comparison to you?
- Do you consider your bank account to be a good measure of your success as a person?
- Do you ever have the urge to tell someone else how much you earn or how much your business is worth?
- Do you enjoy throwing your weight around as a buyer because you are a large account?
- Do you spend more than you can really afford on transportation, clothes, jewelry, hair, and personal-care items?
- Do you get a special high when you tell people your address?
- Do you enjoy the surprise on people's faces when they see the Ph.D. after your name on your business card?
- Have you ever gotten a job because of your looks? Are you aware that physically attractive

people are often considered to be brighter, more personable, and more capable than their less attractive colleagues? Does this fact please you?

The causes of pride flourish in the workplace due to the very nature of the role our jobs play in defining our lives and success, as measured by man. Pride comes from control, power, skill, accomplishments, praise, wealth, and appearance — all matters often noted on the job. In fact, twice a year in formal appraisals, employees are asked to account for many of these things in their past performance and are rated on how they measure up.

If the previous questions lead you to discover that you do have seeds (or great big vines) of pride in your life, what can you expect in your job?

According to the Scriptures, pride leads to conflict. Someone's rights will always be in danger of violation — parking rights, telephone rights, space rights, schedule rights, confidentiality rights, cafeteria rights, meeting-invitation rights. There will be much pettiness, argument, and sullenness.

Some people so accustomed to the deference paid them in one setting can't adjust when they change situations or "platforms." Corporate leaders and even pastors at times feel so threatened when they assume a new job that they begin to replace everyone around them that they perceive to be a threat to their position at center stage. The inevitable outward conflict mirrors their inward conflict over their opinion of themselves and others' opinion of them.

Pride causes confidence in ourselves rather than in God and presumption of the future. We begin to feel that we can make it with or without God. We assume that our security is in our accomplishments and job and, therefore, under our control.

Early in his career, a friend of mine would have been the first to admit that God had fostered his success in his plumbing business. Always careful to give God the credit, he shaped a large, successful company. But as his self-confidence grew, so did his trouble. He began to flaunt his wealth on extravagances that few Fortune 500 CEOs enjoyed as heads of billion-dollar corporations. Within two short years, he landed in bankruptcy—a bankruptcy that by logical analysis should not have happened. Unfortunately, his fast ride with pride isn't all that uncommon in our entrepreneurial arena.

Pride causes mutterings and complaints against God. We begin to ask questions such as: "How come I didn't get the same promotion as Joe?" "How dare God do this to me?" "What did I ever do to deserve this?" "Why am I working harder than anybody around here? Look where it gets me." In other words, we decide that God isn't fair.

Pride causes us to look down on other people, particularly those who are more spiritual than we are and those who are poorer. We feel superior to the person at the next desk and come to such conclusions as, "He's a real fanatic about religion, isn't he?" "He takes the interpretation of the Bible a little too far to be practical, doesn't he?" "Her hard luck is really her own fault. She should have known better." "These employees don't really expect more

money; after all, they've always lived hand-to-mouth."
"I got a good job and educated myself; why can't she?"

Pride leads to self-deceit and blindness about our own shortcomings. New in the business of speaking and training back in 1980, I latched onto every opportunity I could to learn about the industry. One evening at the Dallas airport, I just happened to spot an older, more established trainer in the crowd around baggage claim. We began to talk.

She asked, "How are things going in your new business?"

Thrilled that she'd asked, I shared my good news. "Great. In fact, I'm going to Washington now. They selected me to speak at the national ASTD conference."

"Oh," she said. "I'm certainly glad *I* don't have to do that sort of thing anymore."

My sails collapsed. "What do you mean?"

"Oh, people just steal your materials. Beginners like you, I'm sure, find it beneficial and good PR, but I'm in a position not to have to do those kinds of things anymore."

With sagging spirit, I boarded the plane. So the "honor" wasn't such an honor after all? Well, I decided to make the most of it and learn what I could anyway while attending the convention.

Within three years after that conversation, that woman was all but out of business. Her pride had blinded her to the need to update her skills and information and improve on the services she offered to clients in a competitive world.

How do you know if you suffer from pride? Pride surfaces in situations and feelings such as these: "The company should be really grateful that they have me. Not many people work as hard and know the job as well as I do." We gloss over the seriousness of weaknesses pointed out in our performance appraisals. We tend to blame others — the secretary, the marketing department, the "corporate culture" — for the projects that don't turn out as well as we had planned. We tend to turn positive-thinking tenets into self-justification for stagnation: "I focus on what I do well; the rest doesn't matter."

Finally, unhalted pride eventually brings us down. The payoff is humiliation. Awards begin to go to someone else. Senior management passes us by for bonuses and promotions.

Profits turn to losses. Looks and good health fail. The truth of our own shortcomings and failures comes to the light of day. Others look to us as an example of what *not* to do.

Those who shun God's humility must soon learn to live with their own humiliation. If you doubt the results of pride on the basis of what you see in your office today, tune in to the careers of the proud twenty years down the road.

For Further Reflection:

> Then you say in your heart, "My power and the might of my hand have gained me this wealth." And you shall remember the LORD your God, for it is He who gives you power to get wealth, that He may establish His covenant which He swore to your fathers, as it is this day. Then it shall be, if you by any means forget the LORD your God,

and follow other gods, and serve them and worship them,
I testify against you this day that you shall surely perish.
(Deut. 8:17–19)

Gold and silver are tested in a red-hot furnace, but we
are tested by praise. (Prov. 27:21 CEV)

By pride comes nothing but strife,
But with the well-advised is wisdom. (Prov. 13:10)

When pride comes, then comes shame;
But with the humble is wisdom. (Prov. 11:2)

Pride goes before destruction,
And a haughty spirit before a fall. (Prov. 16:18)

Therefore pride serves as their necklace;
Violence covers them like a garment.
Their eyes bulge with abundance;
They have more than heart could wish.
They scoff and speak wickedly concerning oppression;
They speak loftily.
They set their mouth against the heavens,
And their tongue walks through the earth. (Ps. 73:6–9)

The pride of your heart has deceived you. (Obad. 3)

The Pharisee stood and prayed thus with himself, "God,
I thank You, that I am not like other men — extortioners,
unjust, adulterers, or even as this tax collector. I fast
twice a week; I give tithes of all that I possess." And the
tax collector, standing afar off, would not so much as
raise his eyes to heaven, but beat his breast, saying, "God

be merciful to me a sinner!" I tell you, this man went down to his house justified rather than the other; for everyone who exalts himself will be humbled, and he who humbles himself will be exalted. (Luke 18:11–14)

Everyone proud in heart is an abomination to the LORD;
Though they join forces, none will go unpunished.
(Prov. 16:5)

The fear of the LORD is to hate evil;
Pride and arrogance and the evil way
And the perverse mouth I hate. (Prov. 8:13)

Don't try to seem important in the court of a ruler.
It's better for the ruler to give you a high position than for you to be embarrassed in front of royal officials.
(Prov. 25:6–7 CEV)

Showing respect to the LORD will make you wise, and being humble will bring honor to you. (Prov. 15:33 CEV)

Better to be of a humble spirit with the lowly,
Than to divide the spoil with the proud. (Prov. 16:19)

Toward the scorners he is scornful, but to the humble he shows favor.
The wise will inherit honor, but stubborn fools, disgrace.
(Prov. 3:34–35 NRSV)

He who is of a proud heart stirs up strife,
But he who trusts in the LORD will be prospered.
(Prov. 28:25)

Priorities: Seeking the Kingdom Second

But seek first the kingdom of God and His righteousness,
and all these things shall be added to you.
(Matt. 6:33)

No one can serve two masters; for either he will hate the
one and love the other, or else he will be loyal to the one and
despise the other. You cannot serve God and mammon.
(Matt. 6:24)

A double-minded man [is] unstable in all his ways.
(James 1:8)

Two vice-presidents were recently discussing solutions
to their difficulties in getting project funding. During the era of merger mania, their company had been
bought out three times in a two-year period. As a result,
the rank-and-file manager never knew who would have
final approval of his or her budget requests. In the past,
one VP explained, their managers wrote up a simple
purpose-and-necessity statement that basically said "we
need money to do repairs," and they got what they
wanted. But with the latest buy-out, things had changed.
Past priorities had been repair and maintenance; the new
management's priorities were expansion and governmental

compliance. Needless to say, the managers were having a difficult time getting their budgets approved.

You've possibly experienced your own difficulties with changing priorities and the confusion such scenarios create on the job. Employees feel their efforts have been wasted, they taste defeat before they've even begun a project, and their enthusiasm for the next new idea slides several notches down the scale.

If confusion results from double-mindedness on the job, there's little wonder at the upheavals we feel in our personal lives when our whole being — our relationships, our energy, our time — constantly seesaws on changing priorities.

One month, we decide to devote more time to family, so we arrive home by 6:00 each evening to stay there until bedtime. The next month, we find ourselves attending this or that professional meeting or bowling with the league almost every evening.

The following month, we feel that God is asking us to devote more time to Him, so we volunteer to teach a Bible study class. Three months later, we give it up because our "business is too demanding."

The next month, we hear a missionary's plea for food for a ravished country, and we pledge $50 a month toward that goal. The following month, our kids need an extra jacket, and we wonder how we ever thought we could spare the $50 in the first place. Double-mindedness unravels relationships, wrecks budgets, wastes time and effort, and douses us with guilt and defeat.

So how do we become single-minded?

Not all children, of course, grow up in a household like Joshua's where the father made the declaration: "But as for me and my house, we will serve the Lord." Some of us did grow up where that principle was taught — even in the small matters. My brother and I didn't study for exams or play with our teams in a game if that sporting event conflicted with worship times. We didn't hold back the tenth of our allowance just because we lacked a quarter to buy a favorite toy. Although we as kids didn't always have our druthers about the situation, our priorities were set for us by godly parents.

Adulthood and business, however, have brought us more choices, as well as chances for misjudgment and shuffling priorities. Sometimes I think it's unfortunate that we adults don't always have a Moses to make a circle, an Elijah to build an altar, or a Joshua to draw a line. Stepping inside the circle, up to the altar, or across the line would force us into clear-cut action or inaction.

Most of the time, it's the absence of that clear-cut line that creates our difficulty and stress.

A software package called "Conquering Stress" leads users to take stock of the stress factors in their lives. The program begins with a personal-inventory quiz asking users to rank the importance of various relationships, events, times, and possessions in their lives. After that open-ended self-assessment quiz, users respond to another quiz about how they *actually* spend their time, how they work, and how they relate to people. Many users are quite surprised to see how much their answers differ between the two quizzes.

Simply put, users learn that what they *say* is important to them is *not* where they actually spend their time and money. That discrepancy is what causes stress.

One way to make our lives stable, and therefore less stressful, is to make them one-directional, to hammer out our priorities once and for all. As Disraeli put it: "The secret of success is constancy of purpose." That is, our purpose, or our priorities, must be determined long before we have to face any everyday decisions about actions, time, or money. When those tough decisions come, then it's simply a matter of seeing how they match up to those priorities we've already outlined for our lives and business.

Are God's priorities and our personal priorities in making money always contradictory? Certainly not. The Bible, however, does outline the appropriate whys behind our drive to make money.

One proper motive is to give to God and others. A second proper motive is to provide for our family's needs. A third is to provide for our future needs.

Most of us, if we're honest, are all too well acquainted with the wrong motives: greed, pride, and envy. We have moved from need to greed in the acquiring of things. We are proud of the wealth we've earned by our own hard work or expertise. We envy the Joneses and feel the ego need to wear, eat, maintain, drive, mow, or sit in just what they do.

The farmer noticed the same tendency in his dog. The collie avidly chased every car that passed down the dusty road in front of their farm. The farmer couldn't help but wonder what the dog would do with the car if he ever caught it.

Routinely, we need to stop ourselves to ask what we're chasing. What will we do with "it" whenever we catch it? After all, how much money do we really need?

Such inappropriate motives for working put us in a continually stressful situation. We're not doing what we know, believe, and insist is our first priority.

But if we seek God's priorities—fellowship with Him, time and money invested in His work, and attention to our families—the leftovers we toss toward financing our life-styles will always be adequate. God promised it; we can count on it. Bringing our priorities into line with God's proves the only sensible, stressless, satisfying step toward true success.

For Further Reflection:

Do not love the world or the things in the world. If anyone loves the world, the love of the Father is not in him. For all that is in the world—the lust of the flesh, the lust of the eyes, and the pride of life—is not of the Father but is of the world. And the world is passing away, and the lust of it; but he who does the will of God abides forever. (1 John 2:15–17)

I know your works, that you are neither cold nor hot. I could wish you were cold or hot. So then, because you are lukewarm, and neither cold nor hot, I will vomit you out of My mouth. (Rev. 3:15–16)

When you have eaten and are full, then you shall bless the LORD your God for the good land which He has given you. Beware that you do not forget the LORD your God by not keeping His commandments, His judgments, and His statutes which I command you today, lest—when you have eaten and are full, and have built beautiful houses and dwell in them; and when your herds and your flocks multiply, and your silver and your gold are multiplied, and all that you have is multiplied; when your heart is lifted up, and you forget the LORD your God who brought you out of the land of Egypt, from the house of bondage ... then you say in your heart, "My power and the might of my hand have gained me this wealth." (Deut. 8:10–14, 17)

Productivity: Ask Not What Your Organization Can Do for You; Ask What You Can Do for Your Organization

Whatever your hand finds to do, do it with your might.
(Eccl. 9:10)

Having a lazy person on the job is like a mouth full of
vinegar or smoke in your eyes.
(Prov. 10:26 CEV)

Hard working farmers have more than enough food;
daydreamers are nothing more than stupid fools.
(Prov. 12:11 CEV)

He who is faithful in what is least is faithful also in much;
and he who is unjust in what is least is unjust also in much.
Therefore if you have not been faithful in the unrighteous
mammon, who will commit to your trust the true riches? And
if you have not been faithful in what is another man's, who
will give you what is your own?
(Luke 16:10–12)

"I like work; it fascinates me. I can sit and look at it
for hours," insists humorist Jerome K. Jerome.

Unfortunately, many others, although not exactly fascinated by their work, can make it last as long as necessary to avoid whatever it is they don't really want to do.

Several years ago, M. David Lowe Personnel Agency surveyed 200 Houston workers. They asked about the workers' New Year's resolutions concerning their job. The third most frequently given answer was, "Not waste as much time," which ranked right after "Learning more about the company and industry operations" and "Learning more about computers." Resolution number four fell along the same lines of productivity: "Don't be late."

Anyone who's been in the work force long knows the kind of wasted, nonproductive time these respondents were guiltily referring to. Employees call in sick when the weather's too bad to get out of the house; then they call in sick when the weather's too pretty to waste inside an office building. They arrive late when they oversleep, and they arrive late when they get no sleep.

But tardiness and absenteeism are only a small part of the problem. Once they get to their desks, according to productivity experts, most office employees waste at least 45 percent of the day. A study of nonmanagerial employees, conducted by Daniel Yankelovich's Public Agenda Foundation, revealed that only 22 percent of the employees say they work at full potential. Nearly one half (44 percent) admit that they expend the minimum effort to get by on their job.

According to *Training and Development* magazine, three out of four workers say they could do more work if they wanted to. The Robert Half consulting firm estimates that theft of productive time costs the American economy $170 billion annually.

Ask many of these unproductive people if they put in an honest day's work and they will answer: "No, but..." The reasons are varied:

- "Everybody does it. They expect it."
- "At work is the only time I have to do this...or that."
- "You should see what my boss gets away with."
- "But this job is so boring. If I didn't spend a little time socializing, I'd go nuts."
- "Have you ever seen my paycheck? I'm not going to bust my gut for that little dribble."
- "I'm an unorganized person. That's just the way I am."

Whatever their excuses or reasons, employees would probably become more productive if they really took to heart the scriptural admonitions about productivity.

Thomas Edison said of his great accomplishments, "I never did anything worth doing by accident, nor did any of my inventions come by accident; they came by work." Lack of talent or know-how is seldom the productivity problem.

Instead, the problem is no harder and no easier than a complete change of attitude. The proper attitude could even change the legitimate responses about lack of productivity, such as a lack of time-management skills. If a person were committed to improving those skills, there are self-help books, magazine articles, and seminars available to him on every hand.

To bring on that change of attitude, we first should try simple cheerfulness. Cheerfulness gives great strength. During the recent depression in the oil industry, I commented to a manager about the attitude of his employees. "I guess that since so many people are being laid off these days, your employees are just grateful to still be working. I suppose you see an improvement in attitude and increased productivity in their efforts to keep their jobs."

He shook his head and replied grimly, "Just the opposite. Everybody has a grudge. They don't get anything done for sitting around and grousing about how bad it's going to get."

Companies in the U.S. have gone through so many downsizings and reorganizations in the last few years that just the rumor of an impending restructuring can bring on inertia. While on various consulting projects in different organizations, I've observed first hand the malaise that often sets in. I've heard comments like these:

"We're not doing anything in this department until they make some decisions. Basically, we're just staring out the window."

Or: "Oh, me? I've been calling up my old buddies and networking. No use trying to get any work done here. You never know if they might cancel the whole project."

Or: "We're just waiting to see if they let anybody go. No use getting into the project and having to hand it off to somebody else."

When I asked an employee recently about some of his most significant accomplishments on the job, he snapped, "My most significant accomplishment is keeping my job for twenty years."

Sure, fear and insecurity about a job lead to frustration and anger. But when we feel sullen or irritable, we're sapping our own energy. A smile, a perky step, and a sense of gratefulness invigorates our bodies and our attitudes.

If the job situation proves frustrating and stressful, we can also try improving the way we spend our time off the job. According to minister and educator Charles R. Brown, "We have too many people who live without working, and we have altogether too many who work without living." Not being machines, we can't, of course, turn our minds on and off as we would the light switch when we enter the workplace.

But some of us live such dull, meaningless lives off the job, that we come to work to play. That is, we cultivate no outside interests or friends and find that our only source of interaction with others is between eight and five. When we play hard after hours, we also feel like working hard on the job.

Finally, to improve our attitude about productivity, we need to try putting ourselves on the other side of the fence. That is, we should put ourselves in the place of our customer or boss. Do we respond to customers and clients as we would like to be treated? Are we as helpful as we could be in the situation, or do most of our conversations end like this: "That's not my area of responsibility; I don't know who you need to talk to, but it's not me."

Imagine my surprise one Friday evening when I returned from a week-long trip to find three of our staffers still at work at midnight. A client's job had taken longer than expected, and they had all stayed to finish the project. They could have thrown up their hands at the "impossible," but they chose to get the job done — whatever that required.

Productivity, dedication, and an attitude of helpfulness stand out in a sea of apathy.

How would we, as bosses, feel signing our own paycheck? Would we be eager to pay someone our salary for the work we do? Business owners insist that it's not easy to find employees who "work as to the Lord." A mechanic recently explained to me why he had not hired any help and was instead turning away business. "We didn't get any more done when I used to have someone else helping me, because I then found I had to spend my time standing behind the guy as he put the car door back on, begging him to do it right."

Charles M. Schwab, steel magnate, concluded: "The man who does not work for the love of work but only for money is not likely to make money nor to find much fun in life."

I think most employees will agree that those who never do any more than they get paid for, never get paid for more than they do.

To put it bluntly, we say money talks. We pay sales commissions that are directly derived from one's own effort. Those who are productive and suited to their jobs seek out those situations; those who are less productive and unsuited to their jobs want to be paid regardless of the results.

Scripture mentions an even stronger link than the one between money and productivity; the relationship between God and productivity. A higher motivation for the Christian is to work "as to the Lord" (Col. 3:23). When was the last time you worked eight to five with the awareness that God was looking over your shoulder? If we did that, we might all take on a new perspective about productivity.

For Further Reflection:

And whatever you do in word or deed, do all in the name of the Lord Jesus, giving thanks to God the Father through Him. (Col. 3:17)

Bondservants, obey in all things your masters according to the flesh, not with eyeservice, as men-pleasers, but in sincerity of heart, fearing God. And whatever you do, do it heartily, as to the Lord and not to men, knowing that from the Lord you will receive the reward of the inheritance; for you serve the Lord Christ. (Col. 3:22–24)

You lazy people can learn by watching an anthill. Ants don't have leaders, but they store up food during harvest season. (Prov. 6:6–8 CEV)

The appetite of the lazy craves, and gets nothing, while the appetite of the diligent is richly supplied. (Prov. 13:4 NRSV)

Being lazy is like walking in a thorn patch, but everyone who does right walks on a smooth road. (Prov. 15:19 CEV)

Laziness brings on a deep sleep; an idle person will suffer hunger. (Prov. 19:15 NRSV)

Don't be so lazy that you say, "If I go to work, a lion will eat me!" (Prov. 22:13 CEV)

A messenger you can trust is just as refreshing as cool water in summer. (Prov. 25:13 CEV)

He who has a slack hand becomes poor,
But the hand of the diligent makes rich. (Prov. 10:4)

Keeping the Sabbath and Your Sanity

Remember the Sabbath day, to keep it holy. Six days you shall labor and do all your work.

(Ex. 20:8–9)

If you keep the Sabbath holy, not having your own fun and business on that day, but enjoying the Sabbath and speaking of it with delight as the Lord's holy day, and honoring the Lord in what you do, not following your own desires and pleasure, nor talking idly — then the Lord will be your delight, and I will see to it that you ride high, and get your full share of the blessings I promised to Jacob, your father. The Lord has spoken.

(Isaiah 58:13 TLB)

"For the Son of Man is lord of the sabbath." He left that place and entered their synagogue; a man was there with a withered hand, and they asked him, "Is it lawful to cure on the sabbath?" so that they might accuse him. He said to them, "Suppose one of you has only one sheep and it falls into a pit on the sabbath; will you not lay hold of it and lift it out? How much more valuable is a human being than a sheep! So it is lawful to do good on the sabbath."

(Matt. 12:8–12 NRSV)

Richard Magnussen, CEO of an Ontario furniture manufacturing company, had to answer a tough question from one of his managers. The employee had noticed that Magnussen seemed to put a lot of emphasis on his relationship to God and had expressed a desire to run his business on biblical principles. But the manager was puzzled: "If you're following biblical principles around here, then why do we participate in trade shows on Sunday?"

Taken back by the apparent inconsistency, Magnussen didn't have an answer for his employee. Instead, he went home to think things over. Year after year, his company had participated in the four annual trade exhibits at which most of the year's business was generated. He thought back to his beginnings, when his company was doing only $29,000 in annual sales. Since that beginning, he'd become much more aware of God's claim on his life and had become a deacon, a community leader, and even a Saturday seminar leader on biblical business principles.

But he still had no answer for the manager who asked why he opened his trade booth on Sunday. The only conclusion he came to, after much prayer, was that he shouldn't open. Although not legalistic about Sunday observance, he regretted putting his employees in a position of having to work rather than worship on that day.

So, even with the industry in a slump and fearing a big financial loss because 70 percent of their orders were written on Sundays, Magnussen hung a closed sign on his trade-show booth. The sign simply stated that because he wanted to keep the Lord's Day holy, he could not open for business that day. He apologized for the inconvenience and asked retailers to please stop by again on Monday.

To his surprise, they did. A long line waited as he approached his exhibit on Monday morning. As one of his customers told him, "I don't agree with your ideas, but I respect a man of integrity. That's the kind of man I want to do business with." On that first Monday after the Sunday closing, his company wrote over 30 percent more orders than usual for that day. Within months of that trade show, his furniture was back-ordered nine months, and he had to build a new manufacturing plant. The company paid cash for the plant!

The following year, a survey of Canadian companies based on gross profit per dollar listed the second-place company with a 10 percent profit on the dollar. Magnussen's company came in first place, with a 30 percent profit on the dollar.

God honors those who honor Him.

We create our own messes when we *don't* honor Him. A friend of mine phoned to say that she wouldn't see me in Bible study on Sunday morning because she and her husband had some work that simply must be done on a new software package he was developing for the gas industry. The following Sunday, when she returned to church, I asked her how her week had gone. She smiled sheepishly: "Not too good. We spent from Monday until Thursday trying to get ourselves out of the mess that we made by working last Sunday."

So why do we have God's command to keep His day holy? For one thing, He knew we needed the rest. A pastor friend of mine used to say that you could take your Sundays one day at a time or you could take them all at once in the hospital. Stress-management experts are confirming what God knew all along: Our bodies and minds need time to lie fallow for a while each week, so that we can be productive when we do work.

A member of our college group at church took that admonition about rest seriously. Every Sunday morning, she dragged herself to Bible study with droopy eyes. "The only way I can get myself out of bed Sunday morning is to remind myself that by 12:30 P.M. I'll be back in bed." It was literally a Sunday afternoon ritual that she slept five hours to prepare for the next week.

But as theologian David Swing points out, "Rest is valuable only so far as it is a contrast. Pursued as an end, it becomes a most pitiable condition." The Lord's day is also for doing good.

Observing a list of *don'ts,* as the Pharisees did, is always easier than observing a list of *do's.* But Jesus said that He came not to destroy the law, but to add to it. His additional interpretation that the Lord's Day was meant for our use in doing good gives a positive, active twist to the earlier commandment. How often do we go one step further than rest and actually do good things for others on Sundays?

Finally, Sundays are for thought, for reflection on God and His will for our lives and businesses. To many people, time for thought is time for guilt, emptiness, even pain. Nineteenth-century lawyer and financier Owen D. Young observed: "Leisure is pain; take off our chariot wheels and how heavily we drag the load of life. It is our

curse, like that of Cain; it makes us wander earth around
to fly that tyrant, thought."

When is the last time you spent time on Sundays with
nothing to distract you but thought? Try it. Clear your mind,
have pen and paper ready, and focus on what God might
have to say to you about your work, your relationships, your
personality, your attitude, your plans for the future.

If Sundays bring such emptiness that we need our
work to mask it, we should immediately investigate
further. What else in our life needs attention to bring us
into a right relationship with God?

Sorting our Sundays from the other six days while
assembling ourselves with other believers to worship is
a good place to start.

For Further Reflection:

> You shall keep My Sabbaths and reverence My sanctu-
> ary: I am the LORD. (Lev. 19:30)

> Observe the Sabbath day, to keep it holy, as the LORD
> your God commanded you. (Deut. 5:12)

> The women who had come with him from Galilee fol-
> lowed, and they saw the tomb and how his body was laid.
> Then they returned, and prepared spices and ointments.
> On the sabbath they rested according to the command-
> ment. (Luke 23:55–56 NRSV)

> Not forsaking the assembling of ourselves together, as
> is the manner of some, but exhorting one another, and
> so much the more as you see the Day approaching.
> (Heb. 10:25)

Sales Techniques from the Apostle Paul

But I do not count my life of any value to myself, if only I may finish my course and the ministry that I received from the Lord Jesus, to testify to the good news of God's grace.... Therefore I declare to you this day that I am not responsible for the blood of any of you, for I did not shrink from declaring to you the whole purpose of God.

(Acts 20:24, 26–27 NRSV)

Few salespeople are as sold on their company, their product, or their career goals as the Apostle Paul was on his mission in life. That's understandable, of course; Paul's goals were far more worthy than any such earthly pursuits. Nevertheless, most of us can pick up a few pointers from his persuasive manner and apply them to our own business efforts.

First of all, Paul kept people foremost in his mind. They were important to him, and he remembered their names. In chapter sixteen of his letter to the Romans, he called thirty-two people by name in passing on his greetings to them! Did you ever wonder why he didn't just say, "Tell everybody hello"? People's names are music to their ears. When you call someone by name, you single him out from the crowd and assure him that he is individually special to you.

Yet, how many times do we receive thank-you or congratulatory memos in the office addressed "To all department personnel"? Such a blanket reference defeats the purpose of the whole commendation. How many sales letters have you received that take four paragraphs to tell you all about the writer's company and only one paragraph to discuss your needs, as the customer?

Persuasive people remember names and treat individuals to the attention they deserve. They focus their attention on the coworker's or the customer's needs and interests.

Second, Paul started on common ground with his listeners, taking a positive rather than a negative tone. In his address on Mars Hill, he began with a compliment: "Athenians, I see how extremely religious you are in every way" (Acts 17:22 NRSV). A little later in that same address, he agreed with and quoted one of their own poets about the nature of God: "In him we live and move and have our being" (Acts 17:28 NRSV). These people were capable, Paul implied, of deep thought and intellectual pursuits, needing only to explore their ideas to their ultimate and complete truth.

Later in his defense toward Governor Felix, he expressed a positive, complimentary attitude about his judge's experience: "I cheerfully make my defense, knowing that for many years you have been a judge over this nation" (Acts 24:10 NRSV).

In other words, on both these occasions, Paul did not imply to his listeners that they were unenlightened fools, but rather that they were intelligent people who would make the right decisions, if given all the facts.

Many people in a sales situation, particularly those sitting around a conference table with clients or coworkers, cast their positive good ideas in a negative shadow: "Listen, I've got a better way to do that. You're spending about 50 percent more time on that project than necessary." Such a negative comment isn't nearly as persuasive and readily accepted as, "Would you be interested in an idea that I think can increase your productivity by 50 percent?"

Persuasive people are careful about how they word their suggestions or sales pitch so that their listeners don't feel put down before accepting what they say or doing what they suggest.

A third important aspect of Paul's effectiveness was his sincerity. "I do my best always to have a clear conscience toward God and all people" (Acts 24:16 NRSV). That belief in the truth of what he preached came from personal experience. His defense before his own Jewish brothers (Acts 22) rang with the sincerity of his convictions because of the changes in his own life — his thinking, his attitude, his behavior, his goals.

Have you ever wondered how much more effective TV testimonials would be if the viewer knew the celebrity wasn't being paid to tout the product? If we knew Chris Evert really used Nuprin™? If Larry Bird really ate at McDonald's™?

Although advertisers know that big-name testimonials sell products, they would agree that all the paid commercials in the world aren't nearly as persuasive as one candid shot of the President of the United States or America's favorite pro football quarterback using their product or service.

Sincerity counts. In the conference room, at the podium, in the classroom. Listeners even react to sincerity over the phone lines; callers who sound like they're reading a planned script are often answered with a click and a dial tone.

No matter that it's a cliché, persuasive people practice what they preach.

Fourth, Paul was challenged, not overcome, by obstacles. Acts 20 and 2 Corinthians 11 give long lists of afflictions and obstacles Paul overcame to keep on persuading people of the truth of the Gospel. Will any rejection that modern-day salespeople suffer ever measure up to the things Paul experienced?

When discouraged, perhaps persuasive people should not ask, "Will I feel rejected?" Rather, they should ask, "Will this ruin my life? Will it cost my self-respect?" Usually, neither is the case.

When the feared outcome is not so devastating, persuasive people are much more willing to continue the process with hope for success.

Some salespeople adopt the "win some, lose some" philosophy much too easily. That is, when someone raises an objection or even a question about their idea, they tend to give up the selling effort, rather than put in a little more thought, investigate the objection, and come up with an appropriate response. No one ever claimed being persuasive was easy. Persuasive people think obstacles are worth hurdling.

Finally, Paul, as a good salesperson, asked for the order. That is, he didn't leave his listeners comfortably contemplating their next move; he called them to decisive action.

To a lame man hearing him preach at Lystra, he said, "Stand upright on your feet." The man stood and walked. To the Philippian jailer, he answered, "Believe in the Lord Jesus, and you will be saved, you and your household." To the Jews plotting to kill him, he demanded a trial before Caesar.

Persuasive people follow through with their ideas, products, or services by helping listeners put their words into actions—whether it's signing a check, approving a procedure or policy, joining a cause, or expressing faith.

In all areas of life where they are called on to be persuasive—with families, coworkers, clients, or fellow Christians—persuasive people:

- Make people feel good about themselves, whether it's by remembering their name or their hobby or their wishes.
- Start where others are, at their level of understanding and with what they perceive as their need.
- Believe in their answer to the problem or situation, and show that confidence or belief by their own attitude and behavior.

- Make the extra effort to hurdle objections and obstacles.
- Ask for action and results, not simply leave listeners complacently contemplating.

Take a few minutes to think of areas of your life where you'd like to be more persuasive. Why not rethink your approach and make the necessary changes in your wording, your attitude, and your action?

For Further Reflection:

> And whatever you do, do it heartily, as to the Lord and not to men. (Col. 3:23)

Speaking of Speaking Skills

You can persuade others if you are wise and speak sensibly.
(Prov. 16:23 CEV)

Let your speech always be with grace, seasoned with salt,
that you may know how you ought to answer each one.
(Col. 4:6)

But sanctify the Lord God in your hearts, and always be
ready to give a defense to everyone who asks you a reason
for the hope that is in you, with meekness and fear.
(1 Peter 3:15)

"The further away your job is from manual work, the larger the organization of which you are an employee, the more important it will be that you know how to convey your thoughts in writing or speaking. In the very large organization, whether it is the government, a large business corporation, or the Army, this ability to express yourself is perhaps the most important of all skills you can possess," observes management guru Peter Drucker in his book *People and Performance.*

The Apostle Paul certainly exemplified one who was always ready and capable to express himself about his faith. No doubt all the disciples, regardless of their formal education, became capable of expressing themselves, their faith, and Christ's mission. Moses, too, realized the importance of being able to speak well in order to lead the Israelites out of Egypt. That's why he complained about his stumbling speech until God sent along his brother, Aaron, as spokesman.

"But," some employees may counter, "I'm not the leader of a nation like Moses, or a corporation executive." Again, Jesus gave no outs because of a lowly position. You recall the blind man whom Jesus healed on the Sabbath, to the chagrin of the Pharisees? What was the parents' response to the authorities about the circumstances of his healing? "He is of age; ask him" (John 9:21). At some time or another, we all will find it beneficial, even necessary, to be able to express ourselves well.

We never know when we will be called on to represent our God or our company or God *in* our company. We, as employers and employees, have to be ready to give an answer to everyone that asks who we are, what we're about, and how we can help our fellowman.

As Christians, our speaking, as well as our living, should be above the norm. With study, motivation, practice, and attention to the examples of others, we can avoid becoming one of the following varieties of corporate speakers we've all heard:

Guru: He knows his subject and spouts off in vague, complex language, trying to impress rather than express. He acts bored with the whole occasion and in turn bores everyone else beyond their need or interest.

Showperson: She is an egotist who likes being in front of people no matter what the subject. She jokes, ad-libs, pokes fun, puts on a show, and says nothing of value. She wastes her audience's time.

Shrink-wrapped Package: He knows what he knows and doesn't care whether he communicates that knowledge to his audience. The audience's needs are of no interest to him. He establishes no rapport, and people just can't "touch" him. Just push a button and he automatically spews forth facts and opinions, without regard for those listening.

Christian speakers should give more effort to the occasion—whether it's to present a product to a customer, a problem to senior management, or one's faith to a nonbeliever.

When conducting oral presentation workshops, our instructors insist to a sometimes-skeptical audience that all of us have the ability to express ourselves adequately one-on-one or before a group. We grow up speaking naturally with little effort. If you don't believe it, consider any two-year-old you know. "Susie, come here. Tell these people what you learned about elephants today." And Susie tells. Or, "Johnny, sing the song you learned at church today." Johnny sings. Only when children get into the school systems do they learn fear about speaking before a group. Fear is a learned response.

Therefore, if we learn fear, we can also unlearn it.

The first step toward becoming a good spokesperson is simply to be the natural person that God created. When our love, concern, and enthusiasm for our subject and the other person come through, God will bless the results. The following tips, gained from innumerable well-known speakers, will enable you to answer nonbelievers about the hope and faith within you, and will also make you a more valuable employee to your organization.

Arouse interest in your subject. Use a startling statement, a provocative question, a striking quote, a statement of benefit.

Plan your speeches, if possible. Most people, regardless of what they think, do not do better when they ad-lib.

State your objectives up front. Giving your audience the big picture first will help them understand the details as you proceed.

Get your audience to participate with you in considering your subject. Can you ask a question? Ask them to write their objectives, problems, or solutions. Ask for an opinion.

Adapt your words to the listeners' needs. If your listeners are lawyers, assure them that pens are perfect for signing documents. If the listeners are salesclerks, explain that your pens come with chains, so they can't be detached from the cash register.

Use the "you and I" perspective. Be direct and approachable with your audience.

Do not try to *impress* with big words and long sentences. Instead, aim to *express*. Use clear, understandable terms; as a result, you will impress your listeners with your ideas.

Overcome language or education barriers by using clear, concrete, visual terms. Why say *monetary constraints* when you mean *budget?* Why say to *enhance personal productivity* when you mean *to help you type faster?*

Use analogies, experience, or history to make your topic easier to understand and evaluate.

Use frequent pauses, to let your listeners process what you have said.

Provide a focus as you talk, such as a visual aid, if possible. This visual helps you plan what you want to say and helps your listeners remember what you have said.

Do not react defensively to questions. Restate the question, to make sure you have heard correctly. Organize your answer explicitly for the question. Then verify that you have answered to the listener's satisfaction. Do not return a hostile answer for a hostile question. You will lose your audience.

Use humor. That doesn't mean you have to be a stand-up comic. Simply be light. Relate something amusing that happened to you. Be able to laugh at your own mistakes. Such vulnerability helps listeners identify with you and wish you well.

Do not plan your gestures. Be spontaneous and normal, with a delivery style that results from enthusiasm, confidence in your knowledge of the subject, and a lack of nervousness because of your integrity.

Read the body language of your listeners. Are they growing weary? Are they losing interest? Do they look puzzled? Meet their needs immediately.

Be considerate of your audience's time. Jesus and the apostles spoke for hours on eternally important subjects; taper your own talks accordingly.

Be real and genuine. Be willing to show your emotional attachment to and enthusiasm for your topic. Admit your vulnerabilities.

To see a nonspeaker incorporate these principles and come alive really excites us as trainers. I recall one tall, white-haired systems engineer, who joined our group with great fear and little speaking skill. When he stood to give his first presentation, his shoulders were slumped. As he began, he mumbled inaudibly, used no gestures, never changed his posture, and avoided eye contact with the audience during the entire talk.

After assigning him to a peer coaching team and assuring him that, yes, someone at his age could become an effective speaker, he freed himself mentally to be himself in front of a group. Four days later, he delivered his final presentation on his technical work project to a business audience of colleagues.

So shocked were they by his transformation that they rose to their feet and applauded!

I repeat: Fear is a learned response. It can be unlearned.

Remember that your words will not hide egotism, hypocrisy, boredom, lack of integrity, lack of emotional involvement, or any prejudice.

Never be at a loss for words when you have an opportunity to explain your product, your service, or your faith on the job.

For Further Reflection:

A good man out of the good treasure of his heart brings forth good things, and an evil man out of the evil treasure brings forth evil things. But I say to you that for every idle word men may speak, they will give account of it in the day of judgment. For by your words you will be justified, and by your words you will be condemned. (Matt. 12:35–37)

The Lord GOD has given Me
The tongue of the learned,
That I should know how to speak
A word in season to him who is weary.
He awakens Me morning by morning,
He awakens My ear
To hear as the learned. (Isa. 50:4)

From a wise mind comes careful and persuasive speech. (Prov. 16:23 TLB)

When a Fulfilling Job Leaves You Unfulfilled

I have come that they might have life, and that
they might have it more abundantly.
(John 10:10)

When you have eaten and are full, then you shall bless the
LORD your God for the good land which He has given you.
Beware that you do not forget the LORD your God by not
keeping His commandments, His judgments, and His
statutes which I command you today, lest — when you
have eaten and are full, and have built beautiful houses
and dwell in them; and when your herds and your flocks
multiply, and your silver and your gold are multiplied,
and all that you have is multiplied; when your heart
is lifted up, and you forget the LORD your God who
brought you out of the land of Egypt, from the house of
bondage ... then you say in your heart, "My power
and the might of my hand have gained me this wealth."
(Deut. 8:10–14, 17)

Commit your work to the Lord, then it will succeed.
(Prov. 16:3 TLB)

Try this pop quiz:

• Name the five most successful individuals in the
United States.

- When you introduce acquaintances to each other, do you identify them by mentioning what they do for a living, where they live, or something they've accomplished?
- Have you spent more of your waking hours this past year on reaching spiritual goals or business goals?
- Have you spent more time this past year balancing your checkbook or teaching your children scriptural principles?
- How many times did you choose spending time with your family or friends over spending time at work? Spending time on a work project over family and friends?
- Where did you spend the most money? On charitable projects including your tithes and offerings to God, or on your own leisure, holidays, and vacations?

Now, consider your answers. Did money and status dictate your answers to numbers one and two? Is money the biggest determiner in your choices about time and relationships? Usually, we are better at *defining* success than living it.

Ambition, the spark of financial success, is the fire that ignites creativity, intelligence, and energy when enthusiasm has burned itself out, and the flame of ambition can't be lit by anyone other than its owner. But, unlike ambition's beginning, many things can be responsible for putting out its spark.

Often, the most common extinguisher of ambition is success. Show me the person who owns every material possession, has accomplished every goal she once had, and is acclaimed by friends and strangers alike for her accomplishments, and I'll show you a person who has extinguished her ambition for the world's definition of success. That person comes to ask, "Is this all there is?"

Often that drive to excel is restlessness. Even God rested on the seventh day — not from physical exhaustion, but from a sense of satisfaction, of meaningful pause. He summed up, "It is good."

Therein lies the difference: Successful people often miss the feeling of satisfaction — they do not feel happy — because what they've done is not meaningful. Their success is not attached to a worthwhile cause or result.

The Dallas Morning News recently profiled Wendy Kopp, a twenty-four year-old graduate of Princeton University, who took the plight of the ailing American school system personally. Before she even finished her degree, she founded Teach for America, a foundation that recruits and trains recent graduates in noneducation fields to teach in America's neediest schools. Her efforts have led her to speak in various corporate boardrooms across the nation, as well as to the prestigious Forum Club of Houston. She even made a cold call to billionaire Ross Perot, who committed to a challenge grant of $500,000.

There's nothing like a worthwhile cause to add zip to life. Ask Wendy and thousands of others like her who successfully champion an important cause that benefits their fellowman.

No one can read the Bible and sincerely doubt that God intends us to lead successful lives; the difference of opinion comes in how we define success.

Undoubtedly, if I took a reader poll and asked you to mail in a response card with your definition of success, I would get a pile of comments such as: "Pleasing God with my life"; "Having a successful marriage and well-adjusted children"; "Being happy"; "Doing what I enjoy"; and "Helping people."

But do you really, really feel that way? Does your daily practice show that to be your real conviction? "Singleness of purpose," said John D. Rockefeller, Jr., "is one of the chief essentials for success in life, no matter what may be one's aim." While my company was recently in New York exhibiting for a trade show, I dropped by to visit my literary agent. After we had discussed a rejection of my latest book proposal and a near-miss subrights video sale, he asked me how the trade show had gone. Growing more animated, I began to tell him about various corporation reps coming by my booth, about an overseas assignment, and about a few invitations to speak at conventions. My agent dropped his pencil in mid-sentence and asked, "Then why in the world are you writing books? Why don't you stop this nonsense and make some money?"

Although I only smiled at the age-old questions writers ask themselves and each other, I knew the answer. Letters and phone calls from readers. Satisfaction.

But that answer isn't arrived at easily. For me or for you, I don't think. It usually takes a close glimpse of death.

A family doctor once counseled a teenage girl who had attempted suicide: "You know," he said, "you could have made your parents and your friends really sad today. They would have cried a lot. But after a while, your mom and dad would have had to go back to work; your friends would have gone on to school. They would be forced to go on with life without you, to forget you."

I think it's this aspect of death that scares most of us, rather than the actual dying. We will have lived, and yet, after we're gone, everything will be the same; our life will not have mattered.

What gives life meaning is not what we accomplish on the job. It is not what we own. It is not who we know. It is not who praises us. What gives life meaning is attaching ourselves to something that is significant, to something meaningful. That means linking our lives with God and His purpose in the world. When we do, we'll find that happiness and fulfillment have slipped inside us when we weren't looking.

I like the admonition of Albert Einstein: "Try not to become a man of success but rather try to become a man of value."

For Further Reflection:

Those who are attentive to a matter will prosper, and happy are those who trust in the LORD. (Prov. 16:20 NRSV)

Beloved, I pray that you may prosper in all things and be in health, just as your soul prospers. (3 John 2)

He who trusts in his riches will fall,
But the righteous will flourish like foliage. (Prov. 11:28)

This Book of the Law shall not depart from your mouth, but you shall meditate in it day and night, that you may observe to do according to all that is written in it. For then you will make your way prosperous, and then you will have good success. (Josh. 1:8)

For riches are not forever,
Nor does a crown endure to all generations. (Prov. 27:24)

Where Was Solomon When I Needed Wisdom?

If any of you lacks wisdom, let him ask of God, who gives to all liberally and without reproach, and it will be given to him.
(James 1:5)

In her right hand Wisdom holds a long life,
and in her left hand are wealth and honor.
Wisdom makes life pleasant and leads us safely along.
(Prov. 31:16–17 CEV)

Trust in the LORD with all your heart,
And lean not on your own understanding;
In all your ways acknowledge Him,
And He shall direct your paths.
(Prov. 3:5–6)

"Why do we always find things the last place we look?" the riddle goes. Answer: "Because when we find it, we stop looking." An equally puzzling question: "Why do we take all our decisions to God last, rather than first?"

Most of us still get our wisdom through an ineffective, outdated method: Experience. We find a lot of things that don't work, while we waste time, money, and effort in the process.

First, we look for facts. But the problem is no longer not having enough information to conduct our business. Rather, it is that we have too much information. With our modern technology, we have access to databases on every conceivable subject and enough computer printouts to wrap the world several times. Knowledge and facts we have.

What we lack is the understanding to *use* the information we have. Proverbs 2:6 says that wisdom encompasses both knowledge and the understanding and proper application of that knowledge. In "computerese," wisdom is an analysis of the printout in terms of recommendations.

When the facts don't give us the answers we need, some of us look to the experience of our older colleagues and our bosses. *Mentoring,* the buzz word of the fast-trackers in the early eighties, meant latching on to a gray-haired God substitute who could introduce us to the right people, advise us of the experience we needed, and, if we were lucky, could create the correct circumstances for our promotion.

But with our more experienced colleagues, just as with the computer and our latest technology, we seldom find all the wisdom we need.

Several months ago, we began to consider doing public workshops. So we collected all the data: What segment of the population would be interested in the course? What mailing lists to buy? How many names on each list? What were appropriate fees? What hidden costs were involved? What was the best month of the year for seminars? What was the best day of the week? Even, on what day should the mailer land on the prospective attendees' desks? Which cities would best support the workshop? How many times a year should we offer the course? We had the *facts*.

What we didn't have was the wisdom to see that even a possession of the facts doesn't ensure success. Despite all our calls to colleagues in the business, wisdom and absolutes were difficult to find. Before we called it quits on the idea, we lost $33,000.

Even before mentoring came and went, H. L. Mencken observed: "The older I grow the more I distrust the familiar doctrine that age brings wisdom."

Some of us look to persuasive advice givers for our wisdom. While the talkative among us are always ready to give us a piece of their mind, they often speak from little understanding. According to Sophocles, "Much wisdom often goes with fewest words."

At last, when all other sources fail and with a trail of wasted dollars and time, in desperation we find ourselves turning to God for wisdom on the job.

Nevertheless, we're welcomed whenever we get there. Our first step toward gaining God's wisdom is to know what we do not know, that is, to be aware of our shortcomings. The Apostle Paul, in 1 Corinthians 2, assured the church members of Corinth that he hadn't dared to show up to preach among them armed only with his own glowing wit and wisdom. In fact, he feared and trembled with awareness of his own shortcomings. The method, as well as the results there, was God's effort.

Therefore, because it was God's wisdom he shared, he had every confidence that the effects of his visit would last.

We, too, have to come to the realization that all the printouts in the world, all the marketing plans by the best corporate planning departments, and all the technical experts available do not have all the answers. Saying that we recognize these limitations is one thing; believing it is something else again.

A second condition of wisdom is to acknowledge God as the true source and to ask for His guidance. God doesn't force His wisdom on us, but James 1:5 assures us that He gives liberally when we acknowledge our need and His supply.

A third condition of wisdom is to live righteously with the knowledge and wisdom we have. God gives answers to those whom He can trust to use them for His glory and the benefit of mankind. We can rest assured that God won't give us the wisdom to design and submit a client proposal that will lead us into swindling our suppliers.

A fourth condition and advantage in finding wisdom is that we walk with wise men. God's wisdom often comes via other believers. If we hang out with fools, we shouldn't be surprised at their foolish advice. In fact, we'll often have trouble separating it from the wisdom of God's messengers.

So how do we know whether our wisdom is from God, or if it's simply the product of jumping on our colleagues' bandwagon, riding a promising wave of the future or using good old uncommon sense?

Perhaps the following observations will help.

God's wisdom makes a man compete only with himself — to increase his wisdom. The world's wisdom encourages us to compete with others.

God's wisdom makes us straightforward. The world's wisdom promotes deceit and manipulation.

God's wisdom leads to harmony. The world's wisdom generates disagreement, anger, and conflict.

God's wisdom treats all human beings with respect. The world's wisdom shows partiality, rewarding only those who have something to give in return.

God's wisdom will lead to kindness. The world's wisdom will lead to mean-spiritedness and even cruelty.

God's wisdom humbles us when we learn of our shortcomings. The world's wisdom makes us proud when we learn of the shortcomings of others.

God's wisdom encourages us to set personal goals and move toward them. The world's wisdom tells us to be complacent with what we are.

God's wisdom brings happiness when we achieve what He wants in our life. The world's wisdom makes us happy when we win praise from our colleagues.

God's wisdom will direct us toward holy, moral actions. The world's wisdom will direct us toward what is expedient.

God's wisdom will result in long-term success. The world's wisdom will result in only short-term profits.

True wisdom is worth the wait. But the next time you need direction in your job, get genuine wisdom in the first place (not the last place) you look.

For Further Reflection:

Do yourself a favor by having good sense — you will be glad you did. (Prov. 19:8 CEV)

The best thing about Wisdom is Wisdom herself; good sense is more important than anything else. (Prov. 4:7 CEV)

He stores up sound wisdom for the upright. (Prov. 2:7)

For wisdom is better than rubies,
And all the things one may desire cannot be compared with her. (Prov. 8:11)

The fear of the LORD is the beginning of wisdom,
And the knowledge of the Holy One is understanding.
(Prov. 9:10)

My son, if you receive my words,
And treasure my commands within you,
So that you incline your ear to wisdom,
And apply your heart to understanding;
Yes, if you cry out for discernment,
And lift up your voice for understanding,
If you seek her as silver,
And search for her as for hidden treasures;
Then you will understand the fear of the LORD,
And find the knowledge of God.
For the LORD gives wisdom;
From His mouth come knowledge and understanding.
(Prov. 2:1–6)

He who walks with wise men will be wise,
But the companion of fools will be destroyed.
(Prov. 13:20)

My child, do not let these escape from your sight: keep
sound wisdom and prudence, and they will be life for
your soul and adornment for your neck.
Then you will walk on your way securely and your foot
will not stumble. (Prov. 3:21–23 NRSV)

The mouth of the righteous brings forth wisdom,
But the perverse tongue will be cut out. (Prov. 10:31)

A wise man is strong,
Yes, a man of knowledge increases strength. (Prov. 24:5)

Worship Nine to Five

My mouth is filled with your praise,
and with your glory all day long.
(Ps. 71:8 NRSV)

But his delight is in the law of the LORD,
And in His law he meditates day and night.
(Ps. 1:2)

My mouth will tell of your righteous acts,
of your deeds of salvation all day long,
though their number is past my knowledge.
(Ps. 71:15 NRSV)

"Morning, George."
"Good morning."
"How's it going, Carol?"
"Okay. How about you?"
"Hello."

And so it goes around most offices at the beginning of each day. Yet those who would never think of stumbling into work without speaking to their colleagues often pass the whole day without speaking to God. It's not that we need to make *our* presence known to God as we do to our coworkers; it's that we need to acknowledge *His* presence in our lives.

Not to downplay the importance of corporate worship with other believers, but private worship outside the walls of the church building is most meaningful. Often, the more formal our worship is, the more ritualistic it is. That is, we can rise, sit, stand, sing, and pray on cue in our churches without ever personally "making connection" with God. If we're not careful, we fall into the habit of letting the ritual substitute for the real.

Therefore, those private, spontaneous moments of worship between 9:00 and 5:00, Monday through Friday, can be as meaningful, if not more so, in changing our behavior and attitudes on the job.

These worship experiences may be planned or unplanned. Like several other firms founded by Christians, a group of senior executives at the headquarters of Stewart Title Guaranty Company meet before work hours every day for Bible study and prayer together. And as an outgrowth of that time, their worship has set the atmosphere for the entire office.

While conducting a writing seminar there on one occasion, I chatted with a secretary before class. Not having met me before, she confided what she thought was a secret: "Let me tell you something about this company before you get too involved here. Things are really . . . different. Some of these people meet every morning to read the Bible and things like that. They even meet to pray over decisions, sometimes. You'll see, it really sets a weird atmosphere around here — affects policies, things like that."

Although her tone and facial expression conveyed her comments negatively, the effect of this group's worship was the same; a witness of their faith. And that witness is ongoing. Four years later, in an interview with a *Wall Street Journal* reporter, I mentioned CEO Carloss Morris at Stewart Title. The reporter commented, "I think I've heard of him several places around town. Isn't he that religious guy that runs his business by the Bible or something?"

Others, like Carloss Morris, use the workplace for worship and witness. Speaking at a Chamber of Commerce marketing seminar, Ninfa Laurenzo, sixty-two-year-old owner of a very successful Mexican restaurant chain in Houston and Dallas, assured the audience that her marketing plan could be summed up simply: Love God, and love the customer. When pushed for further explanation of her success, she expanded, "I love God with all my heart and all my soul. It can't help but spill over to my customers. They know it."

Spontaneously, groups at Exxon and Florida Power and Light, as well as numerous other organizations, have banded together to worship as employee teams. The lift from worship is not only apparent to customers and sets the tone around the office, it also feeds our own spirit.

What better place, what more hectic place, do we go where we need renewed strength and rest than the office? Isaiah 40:31 promises renewed strength — both physical and emotional. A friend of mine recently related to me how her private worship got her through each day during marital difficulties.

"Some days I'd go to the office and force myself to try to concentrate on the job. But about half a day was all I could stand. At lunch, I'd get out my New Testament and walk down to the park near our office and just sit and read and listen and think. If it hadn't been for those times, for that midday lift, for knowing God was there, I think I would not have been able to work during those months."

Like my friend, I, too, have experienced those unplanned moments of worship when circumstances on the job made me so aware of God's care and provision that I couldn't help but immediately stop what I was doing and offer praise.

Not so long ago, I was facing a difficult circumstance in my own life, needing to be off work for an extended period of time. As I began to call clients and tried to rearrange project due dates, it began to look as though things weren't going to work out, and that I might lose several thousand dollars due to client cancellations. But as I lifted my mind to God that afternoon and asked Him to take over the situation, things began to turn around. Two hours and several phone calls later, not only had I held on to the former projects, I had accumulated three more requests for our services, to be rendered on my own timetable.

Was I in a worshipful spirit? You bet! I gathered my husband and both kids around to explain what God had just pulled off!

Yes, spontaneous worship, whenever it happens—and particularly on the job—can be as meaningful nine to five, Monday through Friday, as Sunday morning between ten and noon.

God is ready when you are.

For Further Reflection:

> All day long my tongue will talk of your righteous help, for those who tried to do me harm have been put to shame, and disgraced. (Ps. 71:24 NRSV)

> Therefore by Him let us continually offer the sacrifice of praise to God, that is, the fruit of our lips, giving thanks to His name. (Heb. 13:15)

> Therefore you shall lay up these words of mine in your heart and in your soul, and bind them as a sign on your hand, and they shall be as frontlets between your eyes. You shall teach them to your children, speaking of them when you sit in your house, when you walk by the way, when you lie down, and when you rise up. And you shall write them on the doorposts of your house and on your gates. (Deut. 11:18–20)

> God is Spirit, and those who worship Him must worship in spirit and truth. (John 4:24)

You Can Count on Me —
Unless the Other Guy Gets
the Ten Talents

Moreover it is required in stewards that one be found faithful.
(1 Cor. 4:2)

So take the talent from him, and give it to the one with the
ten talents. For to all those who have, more will be given,
and they will have an abundance; but from those who have
nothing, even what they have will be taken away.
(Matt. 25:28–29 NRSV)

We have gifts that differ according to the grace given to us:
prophecy, in proportion to faith; ministry, in ministering;
the teacher, in teaching; the exhorter, in exhortation;
the giver, in generosity; the leader, in diligence;
the compassionate, in cheerfulness.
(Rom. 12:6–8 NRSV)

O ne of my friends, a former flight attendant, has seen
talent and potential thwarted quite dramatically in
a colleague's life. My friend and her colleague Donna
flew together in their early twenties, and Donna shared
the deepest longing and disappointment of her life. All
during her childhood, she had desperately wanted to
study piano and violin, but her mother refused to hear of

the idea. To be a musician, according to her mother, was to waste her life in pursuit of a financially unrewarding endeavor.

In her adult years, the childhood longing to become a world-famous musician became an obsession with Donna. She began piano and violin lessons on her own, but felt that it was too late to achieve her goals. As a well-paid flight attendant, she lived in a luxurious apartment overlooking the lake on Chicago's Lake Shore Drive. Her rooms were filled wall to wall with expensive musical instruments, stereo systems, and classical albums and tapes. To the exclusion of all other interests, she talked intimately about composers and concert pianists who came to Chicago to entertain, rarely missing their performances.

One day at the height of her distress about her wasted talents, she stood at her apartment window and tossed her Saks Fifth Avenue clothes and all her musical possessions into the street. She now writes letters to my friend from a mental institution complaining about her mother's part in her wasted talents and begging for money.

Most of us cannot blame others for our failure to develop our God-given talents. We are our own worst critics and discouragers.

We look around at the vice presidents in the company, with their still-dark coiffures, their energy, their quick ability to spot a trend that becomes an $8 million line of business. We hear the eloquent speaker who is relaxed and confident before a group of fifty prospective customers who are ready to buy. We consider the engineer, frequently published in technical journals and held in high esteem by her colleagues.

In other words, we make comparisons. And those comparisons almost always hinder our own progress in developing our talents and working to our highest potential. We assume that the other person has more talent than we do and, therefore, that we missed our fair share. We become envious and either give up and/or excuse ourselves for not doing the best with the abilities we do have.

Unlike the car rental agency that is in second place and tries harder, some people draw a defensive, protective shield around themselves and refuse to try at all. They work at nothing heartily. If they don't volunteer to serve on the quality-circles task force, then no one can blame them for not coming up with any cost-saving measures. If they don't do a good job of preparing a new management report, then perhaps nobody will ask them to do it the next time.

Deciding that they can never be the best, many employees settle in to become the least.

Often employees who squander their efforts and talent in a bureaucratic structure think that if they were on their own, they could develop their talent to its highest potential. But as in other situations, man's reasoning is often directly opposite to that of Scripture. The Gospel writer tells us that he who doesn't do his best for his "master" certainly won't do any better for himself.

Several years ago, I received a phone call from a man I'll call Frank. He introduced himself by mentioning several mutual friends, and then proceeded to ask about the possibility of our working together in a contract arrangement on special projects. He had the appropriate academic credentials and a convivial personality, so I told him we'd keep him in mind should some contract possibility come up. As an aside, he mentioned that he had an idea for a book he'd like to publish and wanted to know if I'd give him the name of my agent. I did so, made an introductory call for him, and wished him luck.

From time to time then in the next few months, he checked in with me to see what work might be available. Always I asked how the book was coming, and always his answer was something along these lines: "My own business has been so successful and busy that I just haven't had the time. When I really get out on my own, I'll get to it."

About a year later he called to say that his biggest contract employer had let him go "for no reason." He needed work. At the time, I still didn't have any projects to offer him. Additionally, the grapevine said that Frank had not been at his best when working for the previous employer. When I probed further about the reason for the broken relationship, he admitted that he'd just lost his enthusiasm for the job, that the work was difficult, that the evaluation process was rigged.

As a result of our conversation, I did encourage him to work on the book idea while he finally had some free time.

A year later when Frank called, same conversation. Did I have work for him, he asked. How was he doing on the book, I asked. Same answers. I had no work for him. He had no time to work on his own book project.

Another year passed. Frank called to report that he had begun work for another employer on a contract basis but was "willing in a moment to jump ship" and come to work with us on a project. He didn't like the way his present employer did things.

Last year when we talked—seven years after our first conversation—Frank still hadn't gotten around to that book project. He's been traveling, working, and "first one thing and another."

Check out the cases you know personally. Those who develop their talents, take advantage of all learning opportunities, and give a boss their energy and best effort usually have the same success when they leave the company and go out on their own as an entrepreneur. On the other hand, those who were underachievers when they worked for someone else rarely do any better for themselves.

Employees who do not view their work as a service to God do it unhappily and, usually, not well—whether the profit goes in their own pockets or someone else's.

We should never let ourselves waste time in envying the abilities of others. Our only concern should be to do the best with what we've been given. Whatever it takes to learn, grow, and become proficient at our tasks, God did not give us an option about our performance. We should consider the untapped potential beneath our exterior as if God Himself would be conducting our next annual performance review.

The story is told of a woman who once rushed up to famed violinist Fritz Kreisler after a concert and cried: "I'd give my life to play as beautifully as you do."

Kreisler replied, "I did."

What kind of return is God getting on His investment of talent in you? Why?

For Further Reflection:

> He who is faithful in what is least is faithful also in much; and he who is unjust in what is least is unjust also in much. Therefore if you have not been faithful in the unrighteous mammon, who will commit to your trust the true riches? And if you have not been faithful in what is another man's, who will give you what is your own? (Luke 16:10–12)

> For everyone to whom much is given, from him much will be required; and to whom much has been committed, of him they will ask the more. (Luke 12:48)

For More Information

Dianna Booher travels internationally to speak and present seminars and workshops on the following topics:

Putting Together the Puzzle of Personal Excellence
You Are Your Future
The Gender Gap: "Did You Hear What I Think I Said?"
Communication: From Boardroom to Bedroom
How Will You Know When You Arrive?
Write This Way to Success
Communicating CARE to Customers
Get the Paperwork Off Your Desk
Communication: The Quality and Productivity Links
Support Staff as Team Members

If you would like more information about having Dianna speak to your group, write or phone her Dallas/Fort Worth office:

Booher Consultants, Inc.
1010 W. Euless Blvd., Suite 150
Euless, TX 76040-5009
(817)-545-4532

About the Author

Dianna Booher is the founder and president of Booher Consultants, a Dallas-based training company offering workshops, books, audios, and videos on business communication-related topics such as writing, grammar skills, oral presentations, customer service communication, and paperwork reduction. Her company's clients include NASA, the Department of the Army, IBM, Exxon, Hewlett-Packard, Texas Instruments, *USA Today,* Coopers & Lybrand, Mobil Oil, Chevron, Pennzoil, and Marriott, among others.

A professional speaker as well as the author/creator of twenty-five books, four video programs, and four audio series, Dianna gives keynote speeches and conducts seminars for church and corporate groups worldwide. She holds a master's degree in writing from the University of Houston.

Dianna and her husband, Vernon Rae, live in Euless, Texas, a Dallas/Fort Worth suburb.